Chicken and Poultry
COOKBOOK

by Hank Meadows

Ideals Publishing Corp.
Milwaukee, Wisconsin

Introduction

At last! The complete guide to cooking chicken and poultry from Ideals! Tender, meaty, nutritious poultry is in plentiful supply year round and is a mainstay in fighting rising prices at the supermarket. In addition to delicious recipes for main dishes, accompaniments, and desserts, we've included the basic guidelines to make cooking chicken and poultry a success for you! You will learn the basics of purchasing, storing, and cooking various types of poultry. We show you how to carve a turkey with ease, disjoint whole fryers to save money, and bone poultry with professional results.

Expand your chicken and poultry repertoire beyond broiled chicken. Enjoy the crunchy goodness of Chicken in Beer Batter accompanied by Sweet Potato Biscuits. Journey round the world at your dinner table by serving Arroz con Pollo (Chicken with Rice, Cuban-style), Chicken Cordon Bleu from France, or Chicken Tacos, a variation on a Mexican theme. Find a taste-tempting solution for leftovers in Chicken Quiche, Turkey Tetrazzini, and Chicken Swiss Sandwich Puffs. Your family and friends never knew that chicken and poultry could taste so good!

Contents

ISBN 0-89542-624-2

Copyright © MCMLXXX by Hank Meadows
Published by Ideals Publishing Corporation
Milwaukee, Wisconsin 53201
All rights reserved. Printed and bound in U.S.A.
Published simultaneously in Canada

The Basics

Chicken and Poultry

Sunday dinner at Grandma's house usually meant roast chicken. There is a tantalizing aroma from a tender, young chicken, basted in its own savory juices, and sprinkled with fresh herbs, that no one can resist! Pan gravy made with those savory juices and served over mashed potatoes was part of the tradition. Light, golden meringue on top of fruit pie or baked apples lent a glorious, if momentary finish to the tempting repast.

Fresh is the key to success in cooking any food, and poultry is no exception. You can truly appreciate our forefathers' reasons for giving thanks as they savored fresh roast turkey on the first Thanksgiving.

The following are suggestions for buying, storing, and cooking chicken and poultry. Always wash and dry poultry prior to cooking. Pluck any pinfeathers and singe tiny hairs along wings and legs before preparing. Also included are guidelines for egg cookery, as eggs are featured in a chapter with recipes from appetizers to desserts.

Chicken

When buying chicken, look for firm, meaty, white flesh. A chicken suitable for broiling or frying weighs from 1½ to 3½ pounds. Throughout the book, we refer to these chickens as fryers, although they may be roasted, simmered, broiled, and, of course, fried with success. Fryers are about 9 weeks old when they are put on the market. Chickens used for roasting are larger, usually weighing between 3 to 5 pounds (large enough for stuffing, if desired) and will serve up to 4 people. Roasters are about 12 weeks old. Stewing hens weigh from 4 to 6 pounds and are 10 to 18 months old. They are flavorful but less tender, and are, therefore, most suitable for soups and stews. For serving more than 4 people, select a capon (desexed male chicken). They weigh up to 8 or 9 pounds, have a plentiful amount of white meat and are tender and tasty. Allow 1 pound packaged weight per person when purchasing any of the above types of poultry. For maximum flavor and nutritive value, use frozen poultry within 6 months. Thawing time varies, depending upon the density of the meat.

Cornish Hen

Cornish Hens are a small variety of chicken, which are about 5 to 8 weeks old. They are a cross between a chicken and a game bird in flavor, and are all white meat. Their average weight is 1½ pounds. Allow 1 per person. Use frozen birds within 6 months.

Duck

Most duck sold today is the Long Island variety, 7 or 8 weeks old, which has a heavy layer of fat under the skin. This necessitates a long, slow cooking time. Cook on a rack so that the duck is not standing in the accumulated fat. Prick skin several times during the roasting for a crisp skin. Duck has a bold, rich taste. Allow 1 duck for 2 people. Use frozen duck within 6 months. Thawing time in the refrigerator is 1 to 2 days for a 3- to 5-pound bird .

Goose

A goose should be purchased when it is about 11 weeks old; any older, and it is too fatty. They average about 6 to 12 pounds in weight and are quite tender. Prick skin several times during roasting to allow fat to drain. Allow 1 pound per person. Use frozen goose within 6 months. Thawing time for a 6- to 12-pound goose is 1 to 2 days in the refrigerator.

Turkey

Turkey has become a year round favorite and ranges in size from 4 pounds to over 30 pounds. If you want an 8- to 15-pound turkey, select a hen. If you want a 16- to 25-pound turkey, select a tom. Look for firm skin, plump legs and thighs, and a meaty breast. Allow 1 pound packaged weight per person. Use frozen bird within 6 months. To thaw a frozen turkey, allow four days in the refrigerator (still sealed in plastic) or overnight at room temperature. Do not store leftover stuffing in the cavity of the cooked bird as this is an invitation for bacteria to breed.

Squab

Squab are young pigeons, very tender and considered a delicacy. Allow 1 per person. Use frozen birds within 6 months.

Partridge and Quail

Partridge and quail in the United States are both really quail. True partridge are imported from

England and can be found in some specialty food shops. The meat is very light, with a delicate flavor. Allow 1 bird per person. Use frozen birds within 8 months.

Pheasant

Pheasant has a delicate flavor and averages about 3 pounds in weight. Allow 1 pound of meat per person. Use frozen bird within 8 months.

Eggs

The egg is perhaps the most versatile food staple in our diet. It shows up at breakfast, lunch, dinner, and midnight snacks in forms ranging from scrambled and omelets to main-dish soufflés to cakes and pies.

Eggs are great inflation-fighters . . . 1 dozen Grade A large eggs at a nationwide average price of 79¢ per dozen, is enough to make main-dish omelets for 6 people! Eggs are a nutritious, quick, easy, and economical answer when the cook wonders what to have for dinner tonight.

Try to buy the freshest eggs available. If you live near a farmers' market, you will benefit from the delicious flavor that only farm-fresh products have. To test an egg for freshness, gently place it in a container of water: if it sinks to the bottom, it is fresh.

Eggs are graded on the basis of appearance and weight, Grade AA being the best quality available. Shell color may range from white to dark brown and does not affect flavor, nutritive value, or cooking performance. Store eggs in the refrigerator as soon as you buy them . . . they become stale if stored at room temperature. Do not wash eggs after purchasing, as you will remove the protective film which keeps out bacteria.

If using just the egg yolks in a recipe, store the whites in a tightly covered container in the refrigerator. The whites may be added to soufflés and omelets or used for meringues. They will keep for up to 10 days. If using just the whites in the recipe, store the yolks in a bowl, covered with cold water in the refrigerator. Add to scrambled eggs or use in meat loaf. They will last 2 to 3 days.

Aluminum cooking utensils and eggs have an unappetizing effect on each other. Aluminum pans will darken if eggs are cooked in them, and eggs will turn a gray-green color. Enamel, glass, or a non-stick surface are best for cooking eggs.

Cook eggs slowly . . . high heat toughens the texture and lessens the flavor. Cook eggs at room temperature for best results.

For perfect hard-boiled eggs, bring enough water to cover the amount of eggs you are cooking to a rolling boil in a non-aluminum pan. Gently lower room-temperature eggs into the water with a spoon. Adjust the heat so that the water is barely bubbly. Cook a hard-boiled egg in this manner for 5½ minutes. Remove at once and submerge in cold water. This will make the eggs easier to shell. Mark hard-boiled eggs with a pencil and separate from uncooked eggs when storing in the refrigerator.

Boning a Chicken

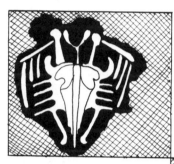

1. Boning is a simple matter. All cutting and scraping is done against the bones—primarily the breastbone (in the center of drawing).

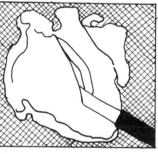

2. Cut down one side of breastbone. Keep knife against bone, using sideway scraping motions. Pull flesh away from bone with fingers.

3. Cut meat loose from breastbone at shoulder end.

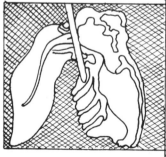

4. Pull tendon (on underside attached to shoulder) as you scrape against it with knife. You now have a boned chicken breast.

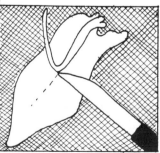

Cutting Up a Whole Chicken

1. Grasp chicken by legs, breast side down. Remove wing by cutting close to body through joint.

2. Place chicken on back with legs toward you. Grasp leg, cut between leg and thigh joint. Break joint; cut around thigh.

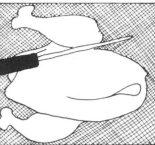

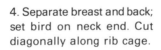

3. Separate thigh from drumstick by cutting through joint, following the yellow line of fat.

4. Separate breast and back; set bird on neck end. Cut diagonally along rib cage.

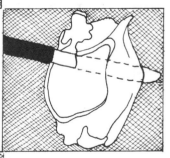

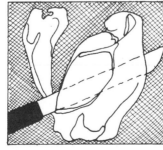

5. Keep knife close to bone; cut along backbone, through neck end.

6. Make cut through V of wishbone. Bend breast halves back to pop bone. Cut breast down center. You now have a cut-up chicken.

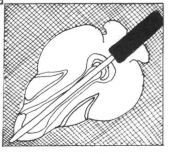

Carving Poultry

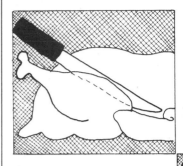

1. Bend leg away from body. Cut between leg and body and divide at joint.

2. Hold drumstick upright. Slice meat, turning drumstick to obtain uniform slices.

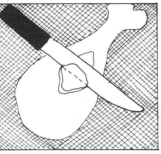

3. Cut around thigh bone with point of knife. Remove thigh bone.

4. Slice thigh meat down to the body.

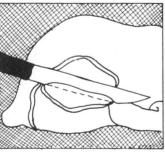

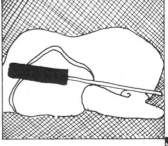

5. Cut between wing and body. Break joint and remove wing.

6. Slice breast meat in thin slices, parallel to the breastbone, beginning at top of bird.

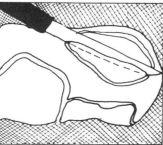

Chicken

Weight as Purchased	Oven Temperature	Roasting Time
2 to 3 pounds	350° F.	1½ to 2 hours
3¼ to 3¾ pounds	325° F.	2¼ to 2½ hours
4 to 5 pounds	325° F.	2¾ to 3 hours
Capons		
5½ to 7 pounds	325° F.	3¼ to 4 hours

Roast Chicken

Stuffing

- 1 cup mashed potatoes
- ½ cup soft bread crumbs
- ¼ teaspoon salt
- ¼ teaspoon sage
- 1 egg
- ¼ cup minced onion

Chicken

- 1 roasting chicken, washed and drained
- 2 carrots, sliced
- 1 stalk celery, sliced
- 1 medium onion, sliced
- 3 tablespoons butter
-   Seasoned salt

Gravy

- 1¼ cups drippings from roaster
- 3 tablespoons flour

Mix stuffing ingredients together well. Stuff into chicken and close with toothpicks. Place vegetables around bottom of roasting pan and place chicken in pan skin side down. Rub with butter and sprinkle with salt. Cover and roast in 350° oven for 2 hours. After 1 hour, add 1 cup water. Remove chicken to a warm platter. To make gravy, skim off drippings from pan, reserving 1¼ cups. Brown flour in 3 tablespoons of drippings. Add flour mixture to remaining drippings and bring to a boil. Cook over medium heat 3 to 4 minutes. Serves 4 to 6.

Try placing a few strips of hickory-smoked bacon on a roasting chicken or capon during the roasting time. This will baste the bird and add a delicious flavor to the meat.

Chicken with Lemon

- 6 chicken breasts, dredged in flour
- ¼ cup chopped green onion
- 3 tablespoons butter
- 1 cup Rhine wine or chicken stock
- ⅓ cup lemon juice
- 1 tablespoon grated lemon rind
- 1 teaspoon parsley
- 1 teaspoon rosemary
- 1 teaspoon tarragon
- 1 cup light cream
- 1 teaspoon seasoned salt
-   Lemon slices

Brown chicken and onion in butter. Add wine, lemon juice, rind and spices. Cover and cook slowly for 40 minutes. Add cream and seasoned salt. Garnish with lemon slices. Serve with vegetable and rice. Serves 6.

Chicken in Beer Batter

- 1 3½-pound fryer, cut in serving pieces
- 1 stalk celery, sliced
- 1 small onion, sliced
- 1 carrot, sliced
- 1 teaspoon salt
- ¼ teaspoon pepper
-   Beer Batter
-   Vegetable oil
-   Flour

Place chicken pieces in a heavy kettle and cover with water. Add celery, onion, and carrot. Season with salt and pepper, and simmer until tender, about 20 to 25 minutes. Cool meat. Shake chicken pieces in flour, then dip in Beer Batter, and deep fry in 375° oil about 5 minutes. Serves 4.

Beer Batter

- 3 eggs
- ½ cup flour
- ½ cup cornstarch
- ¼ teaspoon curry powder
- ½ teaspoon sugar
- 1 teaspoon seasoned salt
- ⅓ cup beer or water

Beat eggs. Add ½ cup flour, cornstarch, curry powder, sugar, salt, beer or water, and blend well.

Chicken in Beer Batter
Sweet Potato Biscuits, page 56

Chicken

Chicken Creole

- 2 2½-pound fryers, cut in serving pieces
- 2 cups Seasoned Flour
- 1 cup butter or margarine
  Creole Sauce
- 6 cups steamed rice

Dredge chicken in Seasoned Flour. Brown in butter. When brown, place in a 3-quart casserole. Pour Creole Sauce over chicken. Bake in a 350° oven for 45 minutes. Serve with steamed rice. Serves 6 to 8.

Creole Sauce

- 1 large onion
- 2 green peppers
- 4 stalks celery
- ½ cup margarine
- 2 cups canned tomatoes
- 2 cups tomato purée
- 2 cups chicken stock
- 1 cup sliced mushrooms
- 1 cup sliced, pitted olives
- 2 bay leaves
  Pinch garlic powder
- 3 tablespoons sugar
  Salt and pepper to taste

Slice onion, pepper, and celery julienne style and sauté in margarine 4 to 5 minutes. Add remaining ingredients and simmer 1 hour.

Seasoned Flour

- 1 cup flour
- 1 teaspoon salt
- ½ teaspoon paprika
- ½ teaspoon pepper

Sift all ingredients together. Yield: enough to dredge 3 to 4 pounds of chicken. Make several batches at one time and store in tightly covered container.

Baked Chicken in Cream

- 1 3-pound fryer, cut in serving pieces
- 1½ cups Seasoned Flour
- ¼ cup butter or margarine
- 1 cup light cream
- 1 8-ounce can biscuit dough, separated

Roll chicken in Seasoned Flour and sauté in butter until brown. Place in a 3-quart casserole and pour cream over chicken. Cover and bake in a 300° oven for 1 hour and 15 minutes. Add biscuit dough to top of chicken. Cover and bake another 15 minutes. Remove cover last 5 minutes. Serves 4 to 6.

Chicken Stuffed Cabbage Rolls

- 1 head cabbage, core removed
- 2 cups diced, cooked chicken
- 1 medium onion, diced
- ¼ teaspoon pepper
- 1 cup cooked rice
- 2 eggs
- 1 16-ounce can tomatoes
- 1 16-ounce can tomato sauce
- ½ cup brown sugar
- 1 teaspoon salt
  Juice of 2 lemons

Place whole cabbage in boiling water. Cover and set aside. Combine chicken, onion, pepper, rice, and eggs; mix thoroughly. Set aside. In bowl, mix tomatoes, tomato sauce, brown sugar, salt, and lemon juice. Drain cabbage, peel off leaves and flatten. Place about 2 tablespoons chicken mixture in each leaf and roll. Use all of the mixture. Cut up leftover cabbage and add to tomato sauce mixture. Place cabbage rolls in baking dish. Pour in tomato sauce mixture. Cover and bake for 1 hour and 15 minutes in a 350° oven. Uncover the last half hour. Serves 6.

Pineapple Chicken

- 1 fryer, cut in serving pieces
- ½ cup vegetable oil
  Paprika
- 1 teaspoon seasoned salt
- 1 17-ounce can pineapple chunks
- 1 cup water
- ½ cup brown sugar
- ¼ teaspoon cinnamon
- ½ teaspoon curry powder
- ¼ cup butter or margarine
- 3 tablespoons cornstarch mixed with
  3 tablespoons water

Rub chicken with oil, paprika, and seasoned salt. Place in baking pan and bake in a 350° oven for 40 minutes. Drain liquid from pineapple into saucepan, reserving fruit. Add 1 cup water, brown sugar, cinnamon, curry powder, and butter. Bring to a boil. Thicken with cornstarch mixture. Simmer for 2 minutes. Add pineapple and pour over chicken. Bake 20 minutes more. Serves 4.

Old-Fashioned Chicken Puffs

- 2 tablespoons margarine, melted
- 2 eggs, slightly beaten
- ½ cup milk or chicken stock
- 2 teaspoons baking powder
- 1 teaspoon salt
- 1½ cups flour
- 1½ cups diced, cooked chicken
- 2 cups vegetable oil

Stir margarine into eggs and milk or stock. Combine baking powder, salt, and flour; add to egg mixture. Add chicken and mix well. Drop by spoonfuls into hot oil and cook for 3 to 4 minutes until brown on all sides. Delicious with gravy and peas. Makes 2 dozen.

Cranberry Chicken

- 2 fryers, cut in serving piees
- 2 cups Seasoned Flour (p. 8)
- 1 small onion, minced
- 4 tablespoons butter
- 3 cups pineapple juice
- 1 to 2 cups cranberries
- ½ cup sugar
- 3 tablespoons cornstarch
- 3 tablespoons water

Dredge chicken in Seasoned Flour. Brown chicken and onion in butter. Place in baking dish and add pineapple juice. Cover and bake in a 350° oven for 30 minutes. Add cranberries and sugar. Mix cornstarch and water and add. Bake for additional 15 to 20 minutes, uncovered. Serve with rice. Serves 8.

Chicken Cordon Bleu

- 4 large chicken breasts, boned
- 4 thin slices ham
- 4 ¼-inch slices Swiss cheese
- 1 cup Seasoned Flour (p. 8)
- 2 eggs, beaten
- ¼ cup milk
- 1 cup bread crumbs or cracker meal
- ¼ cup vegetable oil

Flatten chicken breasts with broad side of a cleaver without breaking through meat. Roll ham slices in cheese slices, then roll in chicken breasts. Beat eggs and milk together. Press meats and cheese together firmly. Dip chicken rolls in flour, egg mixture, and bread crumbs. Fry in hot oil until brown. Bake in a 350° oven for 15 minutes. Serves 4.

Maryland Fried Chicken

- 1 3-pound fryer, cut in serving pieces
- 1 egg
- ¼ cup water
- 1½ cups Seasoned Flour (p. 8)
  Bread crumbs
- ½ pound salt pork, cubed
- 3 tablespoons flour
- 2 cups light cream

Rinse chicken in cold water. Beat egg with water. Roll chicken in Seasoned Flour, dip in egg, then roll in bread crumbs. In a large skillet, melt fat from salt pork. Add chicken, cover, and cook slowly for 1 hour, browning on all sides. When done, remove chicken to a warm platter. Add 3 tablespoons flour to drippings and blend well. Slowly stir in light cream and simmer for 2 to 3 minutes until thick. Correct seasoning and serve with chicken. Serves 4 to 6.

Chicken Fricassee

- 2 3-pound fryers, cut in serving pieces
  Flour
- ½ cup butter or margarine
- 2 stalks celery, sliced
- 2 medium onions, quartered
- 2 carrots, sliced
- 1½ teaspoons salt
- ¼ teaspoon pepper
- ¼ teaspoon rosemary
- ½ teaspoon yellow food coloring
- 4 cups chicken stock or bouillon
- 4 tablespoons melted butter mixed with 4 tablespoons flour
- ½ pound mushrooms, sliced and sautéed
- 2 cups light cream, scalded

Flour chicken and brown in butter in a large skillet. Place in stock pot. Add celery, onions, carrots, spices, and chicken stock with yellow food coloring. Simmer for 45 minutes until chicken is tender. Add flour mixture to stock. Simmer several minutes, then add mushrooms and light cream. Simmer several minutes more. Correct seasoning. Serve with rice. Serves 8.

Baked Chicken Halves

1 2½-pound fryer
Salt, pepper and paprika to taste
Melted butter
Blanched almonds
Parsley

With a boning knife, cut tail off fryer. Cut straight down back. Press on breastbone with knife, pulling chicken in half. Cut out ribs. Sprinkle chicken with salt, pepper, and paprika. Brush with melted butter. Bake in a 375° oven for 50 minutes. Garnish chicken with blanched almonds and parsley. Serves 2.

Chicken and Sour Cream

1 fryer, cut in serving pieces
½ cup chopped onion
½ cup butter or margarine
2 tablespoons flour
1 cup light cream
1 cup sour cream
½ cup stuffed olives
1 teaspoon seasoned salt

Brown chicken and onion in butter. Remove chicken and place in baking pan. Add flour to drippings and mix well. Slowly add light cream. Simmer until thickened, about 2 to 3 minutes. Stir in sour cream, olives, and salt. Pour over chicken and bake in a 350° oven for 30 minutes. Serve with rice. Serves 4.

Hunter-Style Chicken

2 2½-pound fryers, cut in serving pieces
3 tablespoons olive oil
3 tablespoons clarified butter
1½ cups sliced onion
1 cup sliced celery
2 cloves garlic, minced
1 cup sliced green pepper
1 17-ounce can Italian tomatoes
1 cup red wine or tomato sauce
2 tablespoons sugar
½ teaspoon sweet basil
½ teaspoon pepper
1½ teaspoons seasoned salt
3 tablespoons chopped parsley

In a large skillet, combine butter and oil and heat. Add chicken and brown. Remove chicken from pan. Add onion, celery, garlic, and pepper. Cook for 3 to 4 minutes. Add tomatoes, wine, sugar, seasonings, parsley, and chicken. Cover and simmer for 45 to 50 minutes or until tender. Serves 6 to 8.

Arroz con Pollo

2 3-pound fryers, cut in serving pieces
1½ cups Seasoned Flour (p. 8)
½ cup olive oil
2 cloves garlic, minced fine
½ cup finely chopped onion
6 fresh tomatoes, diced
1 green pepper, sliced
1 sweet red pepper, sliced
½ cup chopped parsley
1 bay leaf
¼ teaspoon saffron
1½ teaspoons seasoned salt
3 cups chicken stock
2 cups uncooked long grain rice
½ cup sherry, optional

Dredge chicken in flour. In a large frying pan, heat oil and add garlic, onion, and chicken. Cook chicken until brown. Add tomatoes, peppers, parsley, and seasonings. Pour in chicken stock and simmer. Stir in rice. Simmer gently for 45 minutes. Pour sherry over chicken and rice, if desired. Serves 6 to 8.

Chicken Bonne Femme

2 3-pound roasting chickens
Butter
1 stalk celery
1 small onion
1 carrot
1 cup chicken stock
1 cup white wine
1 bay leaf
3 tablespoons butter, melted
3 tablespoons flour
¼ cup chopped parsley
1 cup peas
1 cup sliced mushrooms
1 cup small carrots
1 cup small whole onions

Wash, dry, and truss chickens. Rub with butter. Place in roasting pan. Slice celery, carrot, and onion julienne style and place in pan. Brown chicken in 375° oven. Reduce heat to 350° and add chicken stock, wine, and bay leaf. Cover and bake for 45 minutes. Remove chickens to warm platter. Cover with foil. Thicken sauce with melted butter mixed with flour. Strain sauce and add chopped parsley. Keep warm. Cook peas, mushrooms, carrots, and onions. Arrange vegetables around chicken and pour sauce over all. Serves 8.

Baked Chicken Halves
Oven Brown Potatoes, page 59
Cucumber Salad, page 49

Chicken

Chicken Catawba

1 3½-pound fryer, cut in serving pieces
¾ cup flour
½ teaspoon paprika
1 teaspoon salt
¼ cup shortening
1 cup Catawba wine or grape juice
½ cup mushrooms
¼ cup almonds

Dredge chicken in flour mixed with paprika and salt. In a large skillet, brown chicken in hot shortening. Place chicken in roasting pan and add wine, mushrooms, and almonds. Bake in a 350° oven for 40 minutes. Serves 4.

Chicken Kiev

4 large chicken breasts, boned
4 ounces frozen butter, cut lengthwise into 4 slices
1 cup flour
2 eggs, beaten with ¼-cup milk
1 cup bread crumbs or cracker meal
½ cup vegetable oil

Cut a 1-inch pocket in the thick side of each chicken breast. Insert slices of frozen butter. Form into rolls and secure with toothpicks. Roll chicken in flour, dip in egg mixture and roll in bread crumbs. In a large skillet, brown chicken in hot oil on all sides. Place in greased baking dish. Bake in a 350° oven for 25 minutes. Serves 4.

Spaghetti with Chicken

2 cups chopped, cooked chicken
¼ cup diced onion
1 clove garlic, minced
¼ cup diced celery
¼ cup diced green pepper
¼ cup sliced mushrooms
¼ cup butter or margarine
3 tablespoons flour
Salt and pepper to taste
2 cups milk or 2 cups tomato sauce
3 tablespoons chopped parsley
1 8-ounce package spaghetti, cooked
Parmesan cheese, grated

Sauté chicken, onion, garlic, celery, green pepper, and mushrooms in butter until tender, about 5 minutes. Add flour and mix well. Add salt and pepper, then slowly stir in milk. Simmer until thickened, about 3 minutes. Add parsley and pour over spaghetti. Garnish with Parmesan cheese. Serves 2.

Chicken in White Wine Sauce

1 2½- to 3-pound fryer, cut in serving pieces
1 teaspoon seasoned salt
¼ pound butter or margarine
5 tablespoons flour
1 cup white wine
Water
1 bay leaf
1 cup cooked carrots
1 cup cooked peas
1 4-ounce jar pearl onions
1 cup light cream

Season chicken. Brown chicken in butter. When brown, pour off butter and mix with flour; set aside. Add wine and enough water to barely cover chicken. Add bay leaf and simmer 45 to 50 minutes or until chicken is tender. Add carrots, peas, and onions. Simmer several minutes more. Thicken with reserved butter mixture. When thick, add light cream. Serve with noodles. Serves 4 to 6.

Curried Chicken

1 3-pound fryer, cut in serving pieces
Flour
½ cup vegetable oil
1 cup diced onion
2 stalks celery, diced
2 cloves garlic, minced
3 tablespoons flour
2½ cups chicken stock
1 tablespoon curry powder
1 teaspoon seasoned salt
1 banana, diced

Roll chicken in flour. Heat oil in large frying pan and brown chicken. Remove chicken. Add onion, celery, and garlic and cook for 4 to 5 minutes. Stir in 3 tablespoons flour. Add chicken stock, curry powder, and seasoned salt. Return chicken to pan and stir slowly. Add banana and cover. Simmer for 45 minutes over low heat, stirring occasionally. Serve with rice. Serves 4.

Variation: After adding banana, sprinkle with cashews.

Chicken a la Sec

4 chicken breasts, boned
½ cup Seasoned Flour (p. 8)
4 tablespoons butter or margarine
2 cups sliced, fresh mushrooms
½ cup sherry
2 tablespoons chopped parsley
2 tablespoons toasted, slivered almonds

Wash chicken breasts and pat dry. Dredge in flour. In a large skillet, brown chicken in butter. Add mushrooms and sauté 3 to 4 minutes. Pour in sherry, cover and simmer 25 to 30 minutes over low heat. Remove cover and sprinkle with parsley and almonds. Serves 4.

Capon and Lobster Knickerbocker

1 cup chopped, cooked capon
1 cup chopped, cooked lobster meat
½ teaspoon paprika
6 tablespoons butter or margarine
½ cup sherry
1⅓ cups light cream
4 egg yolks, slightly beaten
1 tablespoon cognac
2 cups cooked rice

Sauté capon, lobster, and paprika in butter for 3 to 4 minutes. Add sherry and simmer until wine has almost evaporated. Combine cream and egg yolks. Add to meat mixture, stirring constantly until sauce is smooth and thick. Do not boil. Add cognac and serve over hot rice. Serves 2.

Chicken and Noodles

2 cups chopped, cooked chicken or canned, boneless chicken
1 cup chicken bouillon
½ cup sliced celery
½ cup sliced onion
½ cup sliced mushrooms
4 tablespoons butter
3 tablespoons flour
1 cup milk
1 teaspoon salt
¼ teaspoon pepper
1 8-ounce package noodles, cooked
½ cup sour cream

Sauté celery, onion, and mushrooms in butter in a large skillet on low heat for 5 minutes. Add flour to sautéed mixture and mix well. Slowly stir in milk, then chicken and bouillon. Season with salt and pepper. Add noodles. Simmer for several minutes. Stir in sour cream and serve. Serves 4 to 6.

Chicken in the Pot

1 3½-pound fryer
1 beef soup bone, optional
1 large onion, diced
2 carrots, diced
2 stalks celery, diced
½ pound mushrooms, sliced
1 turnip, diced
½ head cabbage, shredded
6 sprigs parsley
1 clove garlic, minced
1 teaspoon salt
½ teaspoon pepper
3 tablespoons butter, melted
3 tablespoons flour

Place chicken and soup bone in a stock pot. Add vegetables and seasonings. Cover with water. Simmer about 2 hours. Remove soup bone and discard. Bone chicken and return meat to pot. Mix butter and flour into a paste. Thicken stock with flour mixture. Serve with noodles. Serves 4.

Chicken Pie

1 4-pound stewing hen, cut in serving pieces
1½ quarts water
1 tablespoon chopped parsley
2 teaspoons seasoned salt
1 cup sliced carrots
1 cup sliced celery
1 cup peas
1 medium onion, diced
1 potato, diced
1 cup sliced mushrooms
1 cup sliced parsnips
3 tablespoons flour
3 tablespoons butter or margarine, melted
Dough for 6 biscuits or 1 8-inch pie crust

Place chicken in pot, cover with water and bring to a boil. Reduce heat, cover and simmer for 1½ to 2 hours until tender. Remove chicken and cool. Cook parsley, vegetables, and salt in chicken broth until vegetables are tender, about 20 to 25 minutes. Thicken broth and vegetables with flour mixed with butter. Remove chicken from bones and discard bones. Cut chicken into large chunks and add to vegetables and broth. Transfer to a greased, large casserole and cover with biscuits or pie dough. Bake in a 350° oven for 18 to 20 minutes or until brown. Serves 8.

Creamed Chicken and Mushrooms

3⅓ tablespoons butter
2 cups cubed, cooked chicken
1 4-ounce can mushrooms with liquid
3 tablespoons flour
½ cup sherry, optional
2 cups milk
½ teaspoon seasoned salt
Dash Tabasco sauce
1 teaspoon Worcestershire sauce

Heat butter in sauté pan. Add chicken and mushrooms, saving mushroom liquid. Simmer several minutes, then add flour and mix well. Add sherry, mushroom liquid, milk, sauces, and salt. Stir well. Simmer 4 to 5 minutes. Serve with rice, noodles or over toast. Serves 4.

Quick Chicken Pie

2 cups finely chopped cooked chicken or turkey
½ cup diced onion
½ cup diced celery
1 tablespoon vegetable oil
2 cups chicken gravy
1 16-ounce can corn, with liquid
2 cups mashed potatoes
1 cup shredded Cheddar cheese

In a frying pan, sauté chicken, celery, and onion in oil until light brown. Add gravy, corn with liquid, and mix well. Press potatoes into a well greased 3-quart casserole and cover with chicken mixture. Sprinkle with Cheddar cheese and bake in a 350° oven for 1 hour. Serves 4 to 6.

Chicken with Green Peppers and Tomatoes

3 tablespoons butter or margarine
2 cups finely chopped, raw chicken
1 cup julienne green pepper
1 cup sliced onion
½ cup sliced celery
¼ cup soy sauce
½ teaspoon seasoned salt
1½ cups chicken stock
3 tablespoons cornstarch mixed with
3 tablespoons water
2 tomatoes, cut in eighths

In a large skillet, melt butter, add chicken and sauté until tender. Add green pepper, onion, and celery. Cook for 3 to 4 minutes. Stir in soy sauce, seasoned salt, and chicken stock. Simmer 5 minutes. Add cornstarch mixture and simmer 2 to 3 minutes more. Mix in tomatoes and heat thoroughly. Serves 6 to 8.

Chicken Quiche

1 cup chopped, cooked chicken
1 9-inch pie shell, unbaked
½ cup sliced mushrooms
¼ cup butter
1 cup shredded Swiss cheese
3 eggs
1½ cups light cream
¼ cup parsley
1 teaspoon seasoned salt
½ cup shredded Parmesan cheese

Place chicken in pie shell. Sauté mushrooms in butter for 3 to 4 minutes. Pour over chicken. Sprinkle Swiss cheese over pie. Beat eggs and light cream together. Add parsley and seasoned salt to cream mixture. Pour over cheese mixture in pie shell. Sprinkle with Parmesan cheese and bake in a 375° oven for 30 to 35 minutes. Serve hot or cold. Serves 6.

Extra-Super Meat Pie

2 tablespoons butter or margarine
1 cup diced celery
1 cup diced onion
2 cups chopped, cooked chicken
1 cup diced tomatoes
1½ cups chicken stock
3 tablespoons flour
3 tablespoons vegetable oil
1 teaspoon seasoned salt
1 9-inch pie shell, unbaked
2 cups mashed potatoes
Parsley
Paprika

Melt margarine in a large skillet. Add celery and onion and simmer for 2 to 3 minutes. Add chicken and cook until heated thoroughly. Mix in tomatoes. Combine flour and vegetable oil and add to stock to thicken. Stir into chicken mixture. Add salt and simmer several minutes. Pour into pie shell and spread with mashed potatoes. Sprinkle with parsley and paprika and bake in a 350° oven for 1 hour. Serves 4 to 6.

Note: For an especially attractive dish, "decorate" with mashed potatoes using a pastry bag.

Be creative! Use a favorite herb(s) to sprinkle on chicken or turkey for roasting. Check lables first to be sure that the herb is compatible with poultry.

Chicken

Chicken Croquettes

4 tablespoons butter or margarine
⅓ cup flour
2 cups milk
¼ teaspoon salt
1½ cups diced, cooked chicken
½ cup bread crumbs
1 teaspoon nutmeg
¼ cup chopped parsley
1 egg
Bread crumbs

Melt butter in a medium-size saucepan. Add flour and mix well. Add salt and 1 cup milk. Stirring constantly, bring to a boil, reduce heat and simmer 2 to 3 minutes until thick. Add chicken, ½ cup bread crumbs, salt, nutmeg, and parsley. Mix and chill. When well-chilled, form mixture into cone shapes. Combine egg and remaining 1 cup milk. Roll cones in bread crumbs, dip in egg mixture, then roll again in crumbs. Chill. Fry in 375° oil in an electric skillet or deep-fryer. Serves 2 to 4.

Leftover Surprise

2 cups chopped, cooked chicken
¼ cup butter or margarine
1 whole tomato, quartered
1 green pepper, sliced
1 cup sliced celery
1 cup sliced onion
1 4-ounce can mushrooms
2 cups chicken stock
3 tablespoons flour
3 tablespoons margarine, melted
Kitchen Bouquet

In a medium-size skillet, brown chicken in butter for 4 to 5 minutes. Add vegetables and cook 3 to 4 minutes more. Pour in chicken stock and simmer 10 minutes. Mix flour and margarine and stir into chicken stock to thicken. Color with Kitchen Bouquet. Serves 4.

Creamed Chicken on Toast

3 tablespoons butter or margarine
3 tablespoons flour
2½ cups milk
Dash Tabasco sauce
1 teaspoon Worcestershire sauce
1 teaspoon salt
1 4-ounce can mushrooms
2 cups diced, cooked chicken
English muffins or toast

Melt butter or margarine in saucepan. Add flour and mix well. Cook several minutes over low heat. Pour in milk and let simmer several minutes. Add sauces, salt, mushrooms, and chicken. Serve on English muffins or toast. Serves 4.

Chicken a la King

3 tablespoons butter
2 cups diced, cooked chicken or turkey
½ cup diced green pepper
3 tablespoons flour
2 cups milk or 1 cup chicken stock and 1 cup milk
1 4-ounce can sliced mushrooms, save liquid
1 teaspoon seasoned salt
¼ cup diced pimiento
1 teaspoon Worcestershire sauce
½ cup sherry

In sauté pan, melt butter. Add chicken and pepper. Cook until thoroughly heated. Add flour and mix well. Add milk and let simmer for 3 to 4 minutes. Add mushrooms and liquid, seasoning, pimiento, Worcestershire sauce, and sherry. Simmer 5 minutes. Serve over steamed rice, noodles, or toast. Serves 4.

Stuffed Peppers

6 green peppers
3 cups diced, cooked chicken
2 eggs
¼ cup diced celery
1 medium onion, diced
2 cups tomato sauce
1 teaspoon salt
¼ teaspoon pepper
½ teaspoon paprika
2 cups cooked rice

Cut peppers in half lengthwise. Drop in boiling water and cook for 5 minutes, then drain well. Mix chicken, eggs, celery, onion, 1 cup of tomato sauce, and seasonings together. Add rice and mix well. Stuff pepper halves. Place in baking pan. Pour remaining cup of tomato sauce over peppers. Bake, covered, for 45 minutes in a 350° oven, uncovered, for 10 more minutes. Serves 6.

Fried Chicken

- 1 3-pound fryer, cut in serving pieces
- 1 cup Seasoned Flour (p. 8)
- 1 egg
- 1 cup milk
- 1 cup shortening

Dredge chicken in Seasoned Flour. Beat egg and milk together. Dip floured chicken in egg mixture, then in flour again. Melt shortening in a large frying pan. When shortening is hot, place chicken in to brown. When chicken is brown, pour off grease. Place chicken in a covered 2-quart casserole. Bake in a 350° oven for 45 minutes. Remove lid during last 5 minutes to allow chicken to crisp. Serves 4.

To prepare chicken for frying, dip in buttermilk or in a mixture of 1 egg with 1 cup of one of the following: milk, water, or orange juice. Then shake coated pieces in one of the following mixtures: flour, cracker meal, cornmeal, bread crumbs, cereal, coconut, herbed bread crumbs, or seasoned flour. For a thicker coating, dip and shake chicken a second time. Chicken can then be fried in lard, butter, margarine, olive oil, peanut oil, cottonseed oil, soybean oil, bacon fat, shortening, rendered chicken fat, or half oil and half clarified butter.

Chicken in Foil

- 4 chicken breasts or thighs, boned
- ¼ cup flour
- 4 thin slices onion
- 4 ¼-inch slices sweet potatoes or russet potatoes
- 4 teaspoons butter or margarine
- 4 teaspoons chicken broth or bouillon
  Salt, pepper, and paprika

Roll chicken in flour. Place one piece of chicken, onion, and potato on each of 4 pieces of heavy-duty aluminum foil. Add 1 teaspoon butter and pour 1 teaspoon chicken broth over each. Season to taste. Bring foil up over chicken and fold edges to make a tight package. Place in 350° oven for 1 hour. May be served from foil package. Serves 4.

Chicken Malacca with Sweet and Sour Sauce

- 4 chicken breasts, boned
- 2 eggs, lightly beaten
- ½ cup pineapple juice
- ½ cup Seasoned Flour (p. 8)
- ½ cup cracker meal
- 1 cup vegetable oil
- 4 cups cooked rice
  Sliced almonds, optional
  Sweet and Sour Sauce

Flatten chicken breasts with heel of hand. Pull off skin. Combine eggs with pineapple juice. Dredge chicken in seasoned flour, dip in egg mixture, then roll in cracker meal. For a heavier batter, dip back into egg mixture and roll in cracker meal once more. Place in 350° oil in an electric skillet and cook for 3 to 4 minutes, until brown. Remove from pan and slice. Serve over rice with Sweet and Sour Sauce. Garnish with almonds, if desired. Serves 4.

Sweet and Sour Sauce

- 2 cups pineapple juice
- 2 cups chicken stock
- ½ cup catsup
- ½ cup vinegar
- ½ cup sugar
- 1½ tablespoons soy sauce
- ½ teaspoon salt
- 1 clove garlic, minced
- 2 to 3 slices gingerroot, optional
- 3 tablespoons cornstarch mixed with ¼ cup water
- ½ cup diced green peppers
- ½ cup sliced carrots
- 1 cup cubed pineapple

Combine first nine ingredients and bring to a boil. Stir in cornstarch mixture to thicken. Blanch peppers and carrots in boiling water for 3 to 4 minutes. Drain and add to sauce. Add pineapple. Simmer 3 to 4 minutes more. Makes about 6 cups.

Chicken

Enchiladas

2½ cups chopped, cooked chicken
    Enchilada Sauce
1 cup sour cream
2 cups grated Cheddar cheese
1 dozen corn tortillas
1 cup sliced olives

Mix cooked meat with ½ cup Enchilada Sauce, sour cream, and 1 cup cheese. Fill and roll tortillas with meat mixture. Place in baking pan, flap side down, and pour remaining sauce over tortillas. Sprinkle with olives and remaining cheese. Bake in a 350° oven for 20 minutes.

Enchilada Sauce

3 tablespoons vegetable oil
1 green pepper, minced
1 medium onion, minced
2 stalks celery, minced
1 16-ounce can tomatoes, crushed
1 10-ounce can chicken stock
1 8-ounce can tomato sauce
1 teaspoon seasoned salt
1 clove garlic, diced
¼ teaspoon cumin
    Dash Tabasco sauce

Sauté vegetables, except tomatoes, in oil for 4 to 5 minutes. Add tomatoes, chicken stock, tomato sauce, and seasonings. Simmer for 30 minutes.

Chicken Tacos

2 cups cooked, diced chicken
1 green pepper, diced
1 medium onion, diced
1 cup diced celery
5 tablespoons vegetable oil
1 cup diced, cooked potatoes
2 cups chicken stock or bouillon
¼ teaspoon cumin
¼ teaspoon garlic powder
1 teaspoon seasoned salt
3 tablespoons flour
12 taco shells
½ head lettuce, shredded
2 tomatoes, diced
¼ pound Cheddar cheese, shredded
1 avocado, diced

In a large skillet, sauté chicken, pepper, onion, and celery in 2 tablespoons oil for 6 to 7 minutes. Add potatoes, stock, and seasonings. Simmer for 10 minutes. Combine flour and remaining oil and add to chicken mixture to thicken. Spread on tortillas and garnish with lettuce, tomato, cheese, and avocado. Makes 12 tacos.

Chicken Adobo

2 3-lb. fryers, cut in serving pieces
1 cup soy sauce
2 cloves garlic, minced
1 teaspoon crushed peppercorns
1 pound pork butt, cut into strips
1 medium onion, diced
    Pinch salt
6 tablespoons vegetable oil
½ cup vinegar
1 cup cornstarch
1 cup chicken stock
2 bay leaves
6 cups cooked rice

Marinate chicken in soy sauce, garlic, and peppercorns for 1 hour. While chicken is marinating, sauté pork and onion in 1 tablespoon oil and a little salt in a large skillet. When nearly done, add vinegar. After vinegar has evaporated, remove pork and onion from pan and reserve. Remove chicken from marinade and dredge in cornstarch. Add chicken to skillet and brown well, adding more of the remaining 5 tablespoons oil as necessary. Add marinade, chicken stock, and bay leaves. Simmer several minutes. Place chicken in a large baking pan and pour in liquid. Add pork and onion and mix well. Cover and place in a 350° oven for 40 minutes. Uncover last 10 minutes. Serve with rice. Serves 6 to 8.

Spanish Chicken

1 3-pound fryer, cut in serving pieces
½ cup flour
¼ cup vegetable oil
1 pound chorizo (Mexican sausage) cut in 2-inch pieces
1 medium onion, diced
1 clove garlic, minced
2 cups chicken stock
½ cup wine vinegar
½ cup brown sugar
1 teaspoon seasoned salt

Dredge chicken in flour. Save remaining flour. Heat oil in frying pan and add chicken and chorizo. Add onion and garlic. When chicken and chorizo have browned, remove from pan, and keep warm. Add remainder of flour to onion in pan and stir well. Add chicken stock, vinegar, sugar, and seasoning. Simmer for 3 minutes. Return chicken and chorizo to pan, cover, and simmer for 30 minutes until chicken is tender. Serve over rice. Serves 6.

Chicken

Chicken Julienne

- 2 2½ to 3-pound chickens
- Salt and pepper
- Butter or margarine
- ½ cup julienne carrots
- ½ cup julienne celery
- ½ cup julienne onions
- ½ cup sliced mushrooms
- 3 tablespoons butter or margarine
- 3 tablespoons flour
- 2½ cups chicken stock
- ½ cup dry vermouth or dry white wine
- ½ cup orange juice
- Peel from one orange, sliced

Rub chicken with butter, salt, and pepper. Brown in a roasting pan in a 425° oven for 9 to 10 minutes. Sauté vegetables in 3 tablespoons butter for 5 minutes. Add flour and mix well. Add chicken stock, vermouth, orange juice, and orange peel. Simmer 1 to 2 minutes more. Pour mixture over chicken, cover, and bake in a 350° oven for 40 to 50 minutes until chicken is tender. Serves 6.

Chimichangas

- 3 cups chopped, raw chicken
- 3 tablespoons butter or margarine
- 1 cup diced onion
- 1 cup diced celery
- 2 tablespoons flour
- ¼ teaspoon garlic powder
- ¼ teaspoon cumin
- 1 teaspoon seasoned salt
- 1 cup diced, cooked potatoes
- 1 3½-ounce can green chili salsa
- 1 cup chicken stock or bouillon
- 6 large flour tortillas
- Shredded lettuce
- Diced tomatoes
- Sour cream
- Sliced olives

Sauté chicken in butter for 3 to 4 minutes. Add onion and celery and cook 3 to 4 minutes more. Stir in flour, mixing well. Add seasonings, potatoes, salsa, and chicken stock. Simmer until thick, about 5 minutes. Divide mixture and place on tortillas. Fold tortillas over meat. Press together, then roll up edges, securing with a toothpick. Deep fry in 350° oil until brown on both sides. Serve over shredded lettuce. Garnish with tomatoes, sour ceam, and sliced olives. Serves 6.

Chicken Stew with Carrot Dumplings

- 1 stewing chicken, cut up
- 1 medium onion, sliced
- 1 stalk celery, sliced
- 2 teaspoons salt
- ⅛ teaspoon thyme
- ⅛ teaspoon pepper
- 3 tablespoons flour mixed with ⅓ cup water
- Carrot Dumplings

Put chicken, onion, celery, seasonings, and water to cover in a large kettle or Dutch oven. Bring to a boil. Cover. Reduce heat and simmer for 2½ to 3 hours or until chicken is tender. With slotted spoon, remove chicken. Cool enough to remove bones from meat. Skim fat from broth. Blend in flour mixture and stir over medium heat until slightly thickened. Add chicken meat. Bring to a boil. Drop in dumplings. Cover and simmer for 15 minutes. Serves 8.

Carrot Dumplings

- 1 cup flour
- 2 teaspoons baking powder
- ½ teaspoon salt
- 3 tablespoons shortening
- ½ cup milk
- ¼ cup shredded carrot
- 1 teaspoon parsley flakes

Sift together flour, baking powder, and salt. Cut in shortening. Add in milk, carrot, and parsley, stirring until flour is moist. Drop dumplings into liquid in 8 mounds.

Chicken Marengo

- 1 2½-pound fryer, cut in serving pieces
- 1½ teaspoons seasoned salt
- ½ cup vegetable oil
- ½ cup minced onion
- 1 clove garlic, minced
- ½ pound fresh or 1 4-ounce can mushrooms
- 1 tablespoon flour
- 1 cup white wine
- 1 cup chicken stock
- 1 8-ounce can tomato sauce

Rub salt into chicken. Place chicken in hot oil and brown well. Place chicken in baking pan. Add onion, garlic, and mushrooms to chicken drippings. Sauté for 3 minutes; add flour and mix well. Add wine and simmer for 1 minute. Stir in chicken stock and tomato sauce. Pour over chicken, cover, and bake in a 350° oven for 45 to 50 minutes. Serve with pasta. Serves 4.

Chicken Morocco

    4 chicken breasts
    ½ teaspoon seasoned salt combined with ½ cup flour
    3 tablespoons vegetable oil
    1 clove garlic, minced
    2 tablespoons wine vinegar
    ½ cup white wine
    ½ cup chicken stock
    1 cup chopped black olives

Rub chicken breasts with flour. Heat oil and garlic. Sauté chicken breasts until brown. Add vinegar and wine. Simmer until evaporated. Add chicken stock and olives. Reduce heat and simmer until chicken is tender, about 30 minutes. Serve with rice. Serves 4.

Spring Chicken a l'Orange

    1 fryer, cut in serving pieces
    1 cup Seasoned Flour (p. 8)
    ¼ cup vegetable oil
    ¼ teaspoon cinnamon
    1 small onion, diced
    1 4-ounce can concentrated orange juice, thawed
    ½ cup ginger ale

Dredge chicken in Seasoned Flour. In a large skillet, fry chicken in oil with cinnamon and onion until brown. Place chicken in baking pan. Pour orange juice and ginger ale over chicken and bake in a covered pan in a 375° oven for 1 hour. Spoon sauce from pan over chicken and serve with rice. Serves 4.

Chicken Portuguese

    2 2½-pound fryers, cut in serving pieces
    2 cups Seasoned Flour (p. 8)
    ½ pound Portuguese sausage, optional
    ½ cup butter or margarine
    1 cup white wine
    2 cups sliced mushrooms
    2 tablespoons chopped green onion
    2 cups chopped tomatoes
    ¼ cup chopped parsley
    2 cloves garlic, minced
    1 bay leaf
    1 teaspoon salt
    ½ teaspoon pepper
    ½ teaspoon sugar

Dredge chicken in Seasoned Flour. Brown chicken and sausage in butter in a large skillet. Remove chicken to a large casserole. Add remainng ingredients. Pour over chicken, cover and bake in a 350° oven for 1 hour. Serve with noodles. Serves 6 to 8.

Chicken Liver Pate

    ½ cup rendered chicken fat
    1 tablespoon unflavored gelatin
    ½ cup butter or margarine
    1 cup chopped onion
    1 cup chopped celery
    1 cup chopped mushrooms
    1½ pounds chicken livers
    2 teaspoons salt
    ½ teaspoon pepper
    ¼ teaspoon garlic powder
    ½ cup sherry

In a heavy saucepan, combine fat, gelatin, butter, onion, celery, mushrooms, and chicken livers. Cook over low heat until tender, about 30 minutes. Add salt, pepper, garlic, and sherry. Purée in blender or food grinder. Chill in refrigerator for 3 to 4 hours. Makes about 6 cups.

Chicken Livers Stroganoff

    2 cups thinly sliced onion
    ¼ cup butter or margarine
    1 pound chicken livers
    1 4-ounce can mushrooms
    1 teaspoon paprika
    ½ teaspoon salt
      Dash pepper
    ¼ teaspoon tarragon
    2 cups brown gravy
    ¼ cup sour cream
    4 cups cooked rice
      Parsley

In a large skillet, sauté onion in butter until tender but not brown. Add chicken livers and mushrooms. Season with paprika, salt, pepper, and tarragon. Cover and cook over low heat for 10 minutes or until livers are tender. Add gravy and simmer for 10 minutes. Slowly stir in sour cream and heat through. Serve over rice and garnish with parsley. Serves 4.

Freeze chicken livers when dressing a fryer. May be used for paté or main dishes. Use within 3 months.

Turkey and Game

Weight as Purchased	Uncovered Pan 325° F. Oven	Covered Pan 350° F. Oven
4 to 8 pounds	3½ to 4½ hours	2½ to 3 hours
8 to 11 pounds	4½ to 4¾ hours	3 to 3½ hours
11 to 14 pounds	4¾ to 5½ hours	3½ to 4 hours
14 to 20 pounds	5½ to 6 hours	4 to 4½ hours
20 to 24 pounds	6 to 7 hours	4½ to 5 hours

Basic Stuffing

¼ cup diced celery
½ cup diced onion
½ cup butter
1 cup sliced mushrooms
1 large loaf dry bread, torn in small pieces
2 eggs, slightly beaten
½ teaspoon poultry seasoning
1 teaspoon salt
 Pinch of garlic powder
3 cups chicken stock

Sauté celery and onion in butter. Combine all ingredients. Turkey should be filled loosely as stuffing expands while baking. Any remaining stuffing may be baked in a covered pan for 1 hour at 350°. Enough for a 20 to 30-pound turkey.

Variations

Apple: Add 2 cups chopped tart apples to Basic Stuffing.

Water Chestnut: Add 2 cups sliced water chestnuts.

Corn Bread: Use ½ loaf corn bread and ½ loaf white bread.

Cracker: Use crushed crackers for half the bread amount.

Giblet: Cook and chop giblets and add to stuffing.

Mushroom: Add 2 cups fresh or 2 cups canned mushrooms.

Onion: Double the amount of onion.

Oyster: Sauté 1 pint of oysters in butter and add to Basic Stuffing.

Prune: Add 1 cup pitted prunes.

Raisin and Nut: Add 1 cup each of raisins and walnuts.

Cranberry: Add 1 cup coarsely chopped cranberries.

Sausage: Add ½ pound cooked bulk sausage.

Bacon: Add ½ pound diced, cooked bacon.

Roast Turkey

Remove heart, gizzard, and neck from turkey. Wash inside of turkey and season with salt and pepper. Rub turkey with butter. Stuff cavity lightly. Bake extra stuffing in a separate pan. Roast turkey in a covered pan with a few onions, carrots, and celery around the sides. Aluminum foil may be used to cover a large bird. Remove cover the last half hour to brown turkey. Test for doneness by moving drumstick and thigh joint. They should move easily.

Cover giblets, heart, gizzard, and neck with water. Add vegetables, such as carrots, celery, and onion, and your choice of seasonings. Simmer until tender, about 2 hours. Retain broth for use in gravy, if desired.

When turkey is done, place on a large serving platter. Cover with foil. Allow 20 minutes "resting time" before carving as the meat needs a chance to absorb the juices and it will make carving much easier.

Basic Giblet Gravy

 Gizzard, liver, heart
1 quart water
1 medium onion, diced
½ cup drippings from roasting pan, butter or margarine
½ cup flour
1 teaspoon seasoned salt

Place gizzard, liver, and heart in water. Add onion and simmer until tender, about 1½ hours. Keep adding water to retain 1 quart of liquid. Mix butter or drippings with flour and brown. Strain stock and add slowly to flour and butter mixture. Stir until smooth and thick, about 3 to 4 minutes. Add salt. Dice giblets and add.

Turkey and Game

To Bone a Turkey

Turkey is nutritious and probably one of the better buys for the money today. Turkey breasts (boned) are available in supermarkets, or whole turkeys can be purchased and boned at home with a sharp knife, in much the same way as boning a chicken.

After thawing the turkey, insert knife along breastbone. Cut along breastbone to bottom of turkey. Work loose with knife by gently edging knife under the meat. Breast should now come loose. Cut thighs, drumsticks, and wings away from carcass and save.

Carcass is then ready for the stock pot. Boil carcass in water to cover for 2 hours. Strain and use stock for soup. Use meat from bones in recipes calling for cooked turkey (or chicken). Breast meat can be sliced into steaks (medallions) or cutlets. Roast drumsticks and thighs with vegetables and seasoning in a 350° oven for 2 hours, covered. Turkey wings can be seasoned, covered with fresh vegetables such as carrots, celery, and onion. Baked covered for 2½ to 3 hours at 350° or until tender, adding up to 2 cups of water as necessary while baking.

Roulades of Turkey

    2 pounds raw turkey breast
    ¼ cup minced parsley
    1 medium onion, minced
    1 pound mushrooms, sliced
    3 tablespoons butter
      Salt and pepper
    1 cup chicken stock
    1 tablespoon cornstarch mixed with
      2 tablespoons water
      Cooked rice, noodles, or stuffing

Cut breast into six slices. Flatten each slice and set aside. Sauté parsley, onion, and mushrooms in butter. Add seasonings and remove from heat. Divide mixture over each turkey slice and roll. Place in buttered baking dish, seam down, with chicken stock. Cover and bake in a 350° oven for 50 minutes. Remove cover last 10 minutes. When turkey rolls are done, remove to warm platter. Thicken stock with cornstarch mixture. Serve over rice, noodles, or stuffing. Serves 4.

Medallions of Turkey Parmesan

    2 pounds raw turkey breast, cut into 8 slices
    1 cup flour
    ½ cup butter or margarine
    1 8-ounce package green noodles, cooked
    2 cups light cream
    1 cup sliced, cooked mushrooms
    ¼ teaspoon curry powder
    1 teaspoon salt
    ¼ teaspoon pepper
    ½ cup sherry
    ½ cup Parmesan cheese

Dredge sliced turkey in flour. Melt butter in sauté pan and brown medallions. Place cooked noodles in a large casserole and arrange medallions on top. Add light cream, mushrooms, and seasonings to drippings in pan. Simmer for 3 to 4 minutes. Stir in sherry and simmer 1 to 2 minutes more. Pour over casserole and sprinkle with Parmesan cheese. Bake covered in a 350° oven for 30 minutes. Serves 6 to 8.

Turkey Cutlets

    1 turkey breast
    1½ cups Seasoned Flour (p. 8)
    1 egg
    1 cup milk
      Cracker meal
      Onion Gravy

Cut breast into eight slices. Pound each slice until double in size. Combine egg and milk. Dredge each cutlet in Seasoned Flour, then egg mixture, then cracker meal. Sauté in 350° oil until brown. Serve with Onion Gravy. Serves 4.

Onion Gravy

    4 tablespoons margarine
    1 cup sliced onion
    3 tablespoons flour
    2½ cups turkey broth or stock
    1 teaspoon seasoned salt
      Dash of Tabasco sauce
    1 teaspoon Worcestershire sauce
    ¼ teaspoon Kitchen Bouquet

Melt margarine in sauté pan; add onion and brown. Stir in flour. Add stock and seasonings and simmer, stirring constantly, over low heat until thick. Makes about 3 cups.

Turkey French Toast Appetizers

     1 cup minced, cooked turkey
     1 tablespoon sweet pickle relish
    ¼ cup chopped celery
    ¼ cup mayonnaise
    12 slices bread
     3 eggs, slightly beaten
    ¾ cup milk
     1 teaspoon sugar
       Margarine

Combine turkey, relish, celery, and mayonnaise. Spread on 6 slices of bread, top with other 6 slices. Beat eggs, milk, and sugar together. Melt margarine on a griddle or in an electric frying pan. Dip sandwiches in mixture and fry until golden. Cut into 24 triangles.

Turkey Hash

    1 cup diced celery
    1 cup diced onion
    3 tablespoons butter or margarine
    2 cups diced, cooked turkey
    2 cups diced, cooked potatoes
    2 cups light cream
    1 teaspoon seasoned salt
    ½ teaspoon paprika

In a large skillet, saute' celery and onion in butter until onion is transparent but not brown. Add turkey, potatoes, and light cream. Cook slowly, stirring occasionally, until heated thoroughly. Add seasoned salt and paprika. Increase heat the last 5 minutes to brown bottom. Serves 4 to 6.

Baked Turkey Loaf

    2 pounds ground, cooked turkey
    1½ cups bread crumbs
    2 teaspoons salt
    ¼ teaspoon pepper
    ½ teaspoon poultry seasoning
    2 eggs
    1 cup milk
    3 hard-boiled eggs, shelled, whole
    1 cup catsup

In a mixing bowl, combine the first seven ingredients and mix well. Place all but 1 cup of mixture in a baking pan and shape into a loaf. Make holes in center of loaf and add eggs in a row. Cover with remaining mixture. Bake in a 350° oven for 1 hour. Pour catsup over loaf and bake 15 minutes more. Serves 6 to 8.

Turkey or Chicken Tetrazzini

    3 tablespoons butter
    3 tablespoons flour
    1½ cups chicken stock
    1½ cups milk
    1 teaspoon seasoned salt
    2 cups cubed cooked turkey or chicken
    ½ cup mushrooms
    1 8-ounce package spaghetti, cooked
      Chopped parsley
      Parmesan cheese

Melt butter in a medium-size skillet, add flour and blend. Add chicken stock, then milk. Stir constantly, until thickened, about 3 to 4 minutes. Add seasoning, chicken, and mushrooms. Simmer for 2 to 3 minutes. Pour over cooked spaghetti. Sprinkle with chopped parsley and Parmesan cheese. Serves 4.

Turkey Mornay

     3 English muffins
     6 slices tomato
     6 slices turkey ham
     6 slices cooked turkey breast
    18 asparagus spears
     3 tablespoons butter
     3 tablespoons flour
     2 cups light cream
    ½ cup shredded Cheddar cheese
     1 teaspoon salt
     1 teaspoon Worcestershire sauce
     2 or 3 dashes Tabasco
       Paprika

Split English muffins and place on a baking sheet. Place a slice of tomato, turkey ham, turkey breast, and 3 asparagus spears on each muffin. In a saucepan, melt butter, add flour, and stir. Slowly stir in light cream and simmer 2 to 3 minutes. Add cheese and seasonings. Stir well. Pour over muffins, sprinkle with paprika, and bake in a 350° oven for 10 to 12 minutes. Serves 6.

Casserole of Turkey

 4 medium potatoes, peeled, parboiled, and sliced
 1 cup onion
 1 cup chopped green pepper
 1 cup chopped celery
 3 tablespoons butter or margarine
 2 cups cubed, cooked turkey or chicken
 2 cups White Sauce (p.61)

Sauté onion, pepper, and celery in butter. In a baking dish, layer potatoes, celery, onion, pepper, and meat. Spread White Sauce over the top layer. Bake in a 350° oven for 1 hour. Serves 6.

Turkey Quiche

 1 9-inch pie crust, unbaked
 1 cup chopped, cooked turkey
 2 tablespoons chopped green onions
 1 3-ounce package cream cheese, softened
 2 tablespoons dry vermouth
 4 eggs
 1 cup heavy cream
 ½ cup milk
 ½ teaspoon salt
 ¼ teaspoon crushed rosemary

Mix turkey with onion, cream cheese, and vermouth; spread in crust. Beat eggs with heavy cream, add milk, and seasonings, and pour over turkey mixture. Bake at 450° for 10 minutes. Reduce temperature to 350° and bake for 40 more minutes. Serves 6.

Roast Turkey Drumsticks

 2 to 4 turkey drumsticks
   Butter
   Salt and paprika to taste
 3 stalks celery
 1 onion, thinly sliced
 2 cups chicken stock or bouillon
 1 16-ounce can tomato sauce
 2 tablespoons butter, melted, mixed with
   2 tablespoons flour
 2 to 4 cups cooked noodles

Rinse drumsticks in cold water. Rub with butter and season with salt and paprika. Place in a greased baking dish. Cut celery in julienne slices and arrange with onion around drumsticks. Add chicken bouillon and tomato sauce. Cover. Bake in a 350° oven for 1½ to 2 hours. Check to see that drumsticks are moist and replace liquid with water as drumsticks cook. When meat is tender, remove drumsticks. Thicken liquid in pan with melted butter mixture. Serve over hot noodles. Serves 2 to 4.

Suggestions for Leftovers

Pot pies
Fried rice
Turkey or chicken salad
Turkey or Chicken Tetrazzini
Stuffed green peppers or cabbage rolls
Turkey or Chicken Creole
Jellied turkey or chicken loaf
Turkey or chicken soup
Turkey or chow mein or chop suey
Egg Foo Yung
Omelet, crepe, or popover fillings
Additions to vegetable casseroles
Turkey or chicken a la king
Chicken and noodles
Chicken puffs or croquettes

Sandwich Fillings

Turkey or chicken giblets finely chopped with hard-boiled eggs and mayonnaise.

Turkey or chicken livers chopped with bacon and mayonnaise.

Turkey or chicken giblets, bacon, celery, and onion, chopped and mixed with mayonnaise and chili sauce.

Turkey or chicken, chopped with sour cream and seasoned with curry.

Turkey or chicken, chopped with any of the following:
almonds
peanuts
mushrooms
celery
water chestnuts
ham
eggs
cheese
or a compatible combination of the above. Add enough mayonnaise to bind ingredients together. Spread on sandwiches and serve with lettuce, tomato, pickles, and potato chips or serve as an appetizer spread with crackers.

Turkey and Game

Roast Turkey Wings

- 3 pounds turkey wings
- 2 teaspoons seasoned salt
  Paprika
- 4 carrots, julienne sliced
- 4 stalks celery, julienne sliced
- 1 medium onion, sliced
- 1 cup tomato sauce
- 1 cup turkey stock or water
- 2 tablespoons vegetable oil
- 2 tablespoons flour
  Sautéed Buttered Noodles

Separate turkey wings at joints. Save tips for stock. Rub with seasoning and paprika. Place in large casserole with vegetables, tomato sauce, and stock, and cover. Bake in a 350° oven for 2 hours. Add water if wings become dry while baking. Remove cover after 2 hours or when meat is tender. Remove meat and vegetables to a bed of warm Sautéed Buttered Noodles. Add enough water to drippings to equal 2 cups liquid. Mix oil and flour and add to liquid to thicken. Simmer a few minutes. Pour sauce over wings and noodles. Serves 4.

Sautéed Buttered Noodles

- 1 10-ounce package noodles
- ½ cup sliced green onion
- ½ cup sliced celery
- 1 cup sliced mushrooms
- 2 tablespoons butter
- 2 tablespoons chopped parsley
- ½ teaspoon salt
- ¼ teaspoon garlic powder
- ½ cup Parmesan cheese

Cook noodles until done. Drain. Sauté onion, celery, and mushrooms in butter for 3 to 4 minutes. Add noodles, parsley, salt, garlic, and cheese. Heat through and serve. Serves 4.

Cheese Turkey Brunch

- 1 cup diced, cooked turkey
- 1 cup grated Cheddar or Swiss cheese
- 1 egg, beaten well
- 6 tablespoons mayonnaise
  Dash Tabasco sauce
  Pinch of salt
- 3 English muffins, split

Mix turkey, cheese, egg, mayonnaise, Tabasco sauce, and salt together. Place mixture on muffins and bake in a 375° oven for 8 to 10 minutes or until lightly browned and puffy. Serves 6.

Turkey Newburg

- ⅓ cup butter
- ¼ cup flour
- 2 cups milk
- ¾ cup shredded Cheddar cheese
- 1 tablespoon chopped pimiento
- 1 teaspoon salt
- ½ cup toasted, slivered almonds
- ½ cup sliced mushrooms
- 1½ cups cooked, sliced turkey
- ¼ cup sherry
- 1 teaspoon minced onion
- ¼ teaspoon pepper

Melt butter and sauté mushrooms for 2 minutes in a chafing dish. Stir in flour until smooth. Add milk, stirring constantly. Add turkey and remaining ingredients, except almonds. Top with almonds just before serving. Serve with rice or patty shells. Serves 4.

Baked Macaroni and Turkey

- 2 cups diced, cooked turkey
- ½ cup diced green pepper
- ¾ cup diced onion
- ½ cup diced celery
- 3 tablespoons butter
- 3 tablespoons flour
- 3 cups light cream or milk, chilled
- 1 teaspoon salt
- ¼ teaspoon pepper
- 3 cups cooked macaroni
- 1 cup shredded Swiss or Cheddar cheese
  Parmesan cheese
  Paprika
  Chopped parsley

Sauté turkey, pepper, onion, and celery in butter until tender but not brown. Add flour and stir well for 2 minutes until flour takes up butter. Slowly add cream, stirring until thick. Mix with cooked macaroni, salt and pepper, and place in a greased, large casserole. Top with shredded cheese. Sprinkle with Parmesan cheese, paprika, and chopped parsley. Bake in a 350° oven for 40 minutes. Serves 6.

Timetable for Roasting Game Birds

Bird	Oven Temperature	Total Roasting Time
Grouse	425° F.	20 to 25 minutes
Guinea hen	350° F.	1½ to 2 hours
Partridge	350° F.	30 to 40 minutes
Pheasant	325° F.	1½ to 2 hours
Squab	400° F.	35 to 45 minutes
Wild duck	450° F.	15 minutes (rare)
		25 minutes (medium)
Wild goose	325° F.	20 to 25 minutes per pound

Roast Goose with Apples

- 1 8-pound goose
- 2 cups bread crumbs
- 1 onion, chopped
- 2 tablespoons butter
- ¼ teaspoon sage
- 1 teaspoon salt
  Pinch of pepper
- 6 to 8 apples
- ¼ cup brown sugar
- 3 sweet potatoes, cooked and mashed

Mix bread crumbs, onion, butter, sage, salt, and pepper together. Cook giblets until tender. Chop and add to stuffing. After cleaning the goose thoroughly, stuff and secure neck and back. Roast 15 minutes at 500°, then reduce heat to 350° and cook 3 hours. Wash and core apples. Sprinkle with brown sugar and stuff with sweet potatoes. Bake about 30 minutes at 350° until tender and serve hot with the goose.

Roast Goose

Rub skin and cavity of a 10- to 12-pound goose with salt and pepper. Pierce the bird well with a fork. Fill cavity with stuffing. Skewer cavity closed. Roast in a 350° oven for 20 to 25 minutes per pound until tender. During roasting, pierce with fork and baste often.

Make stock by placing giblets, neck, liver, 1 stalk celery, 1 carrot, ½ onion, and 1 clove garlic in 2 quarts water in a large saucepan. Bring to a boil and cook until liquid is reduced by half. Season with salt and pepper and 1 chicken bouillon cube. Reduce heat and simmer about 2 hours until tender.

Boneless Roast Goose

Cut goose down the back with a sharp boning knife. Keeping knife close to bone, cut down the sides to breastbone, and carcass will come out easily. Break thighs and drumsticks at joints. Work knife around end and down sides of leg bone until bone will pull out. Cut goose in half lengthwise. Trim excess fat. Pound goose until flat.

Mix 4 cups bread crumbs with 1 cup butter, 1 cup raisins, 1 cup walnuts, ¼ teaspoon sage, ¼ teaspoon sweet basil, and ¼ teaspoon salt. Sprinkle half on meat side of goose. Roll tightly and tie securely with string. Repeat with other half. Bake at 350° for 2½ hours until tender.

While goose is baking, simmer carcass and giblets in water for stock to use in gravy and soup. To make gravy, mix 4 tablespoons of goose fat with 4 tablespoons flour. Bring 3 cups strained stock to a boil. Add flour mixture and simmer until thick. Add 1 cup Plum Sauce and simmer 2 to 3 minutes. Slice goose and pour gravy over. Serve with Red Cabbage.

Plum Sauce

- 1 30-ounce can pitted purple plums in syrup
- 1 cup sugar
- ½ cup water
- ½ cup vinegar
- 2 tablespoons chutney
- 2 sticks cinnamon

Place all ingredients into saucepan and simmer 15 to 20 minutes until thick, stirring frequently. Remove cinnamon sticks. Cool and serve with goose or chicken. Makes about 2 cups.

Sweet and Sour Red Cabbage

- ½ pound fat bacon, diced
- 1 cup diced onion
- 1 large head red cabbage, finely shredded
- 1 cup sugar
- ½ teaspoon salt
- ¼ teaspoon black pepper
- 1 cup chicken stock
- 1 cup vinegar
- 1 teaspoon red food coloring

Sauté bacon and onion lightly in a skillet. Combine sugar, salt, pepper, chicken stock, vinegar, and cabbage in a kettle. Add bacon and onion. Simmer about 40 minutes until cabbage is tender. Serves 6 to 8.

Wild Duck with Apple Raisin Stuffing

3 ducks
6 cups dry bread crumbs
1 cup cubed apple
½ cup raisins
¾ cup butter, melted
2 teaspoons salt
½ teaspoon pepper
¼ teaspoon cinnamon
⅛ teaspoon ginger

Clean ducks thoroughly. Combine other ingredients in bowl and mix. Fill cavity of ducks and close opening with skewers or string. Place in roasting pan, breast side up, and roast for 15 minutes at 450°, uncovered. Reduce heat to 325°. Cover ducks and bake another 2 hours until tender. Serves 6.

Roast Duck a l'Orange

1 5-pound duckling
   Salt and pepper
3 stalks celery
3 carrots
1 apple, sliced
1 small orange, peeled, save peel
1 small onion
   Giblets and neck from duck
3 tablespoons flour
2 cups chicken stock
½ cup port wine
½ cup orange juice
3 tablespoons currant jelly

Salt and pepper duck inside and out. Slice 1 carrot and 1 stalk celery. Fill cavity with celery, carrot, and apple. Place orange in neck cavity and peel in bottom of roasting pan. Dice onion and remaining carrots and celery. Place with giblets and neck in bottom of pan. Place duckling on top. Roast in a 400° oven for 1 hour. Do not add water. Reduce heat to 350° and roast 30 to 40 minutes more. When duck is done, pour off drippings and save. Remove duck to a warm platter. Mix 3 tablespoons of drippings with flour. Add chicken stock to remaining drippings and simmer in a saucepan for 10 minutes. Add port wine, orange juice, and currant jelly. Simmer for 5 minutes. Thicken with flour mixture and simmer for 3 minutes more. Strain and serve with duck. Serves 2 to 4.

Roast Duck with Cherries

1 5-pound duck
   Salt and pepper or seasoned salt
1 stalk celery, chopped
1 onion, chopped
1 carrot, chopped
1 cup red wine
1 cup orange juice
1 16-ounce can pitted bing cherries, drained
2 tablespoons cornstarch mixed with
   2 tablespoons water

Season duck inside and out with salt and pepper or seasoned salt, and place in roasting pan. Arrange celery, onion, and carrot pieces around duck. Cover and bake for 2 to 2½ hours in a 350° oven. The last half hour, pour off drippings, remove vegetables, and add wine and orange juice; do not cover. When done, add cherries and mix well. Remove duck to a platter and bring drippings to a boil. Add cornstarch mixture. Simmer for 2 to 3 minutes. Pour over duck. Serves 2 to 4.

Wild Duck

1 1½-pound duck
1 lemon
½ teaspoon salt
¼ teaspoon pepper
1 apple, cut in quarters
1 carrot, sliced
1 stalk celery, sliced
1 small onion
2 slices bacon
½ cup red wine
2 cups chicken stock
3 tablespoons butter or margarine, melted
3 tablespoons flour

Rub duck inside and out with lemon juice, salt, and pepper. Stuff duck with apple, carrot, celery, and onion. Lay bacon over duck. Place duck in roasting pan and baste with red wine. Roast in a 425° oven for 40 minutes. For well-done duck, roast 20 minutes longer or until tender. Combine melted butter and flour. Make sauce from drippings by adding chicken stock and thickening with flour mixture. Serves 2.

If you are fortunate enough to be faced with the task of preparing squab, prepare it in the same way you would Cornish hen or partridge. If roasting the squab, add a bit of dry tarragon and a pat of butter to the cavity of each bird. Baste with tarragon-flavored, melted butter while cooking.

Turkey and Game

Duck und Kraut

- 1 4- to-5-pound duck
- 4 cups sauerkraut
- 4 carrots, thinly sliced
- 2 stalks celery, diced
- 1 medium onion, diced
- 2 potatoes, diced
- 2 tomatoes, diced
- 3 tablespoons sugar
- ½ teaspoon caraway seed
- 1 cup apple cider
- 1 teaspoon seasoned salt
- 1 cup sour cream

Place duck in roasting pan. Mix remaining ingredients together, except sour cream, and stuff duck lightly. Place any remaining mixture around duck and cover. Bake in a 350° oven for 2½ hours or until tender. Skim off fat, then add 1 cup sour cream to vegetable mixture. Serves 2 to 4.

Pheasant in Gourmet Sauce

- 2 pheasants, quartered
- ½ cup flour
- 1 teaspoon salt
- 1 teaspoon paprika
- ⅛ teaspoon pepper
- ⅛ teaspoon sweet basil
- ¼ cup shortening
- 1 clove garlic, crushed
- ¼ cup chopped olives
- ½ cup water
- ½ teaspoon Worcestershire sauce
- ½ cup white wine

Dredge pheasant with flour mixed with salt, paprika, pepper, and basil. Heat shortening in heavy skillet. Brown pheasant on all sides. Add garlic, olives, water, and Worcestershire sauce. Cover and simmer 45 minutes. Turn pheasant and add wine. Simmer another 45 minutes or until tender. Serves 8.

Pheasant in Mushrooms and Cream

- 1 pheasant, quartered
- 1 10½-ounce can condensed cream of mushroom soup
- ½ cup dairy sour cream
- 4 ounces mushrooms, sliced
- ¼ cup grated Parmesan cheese
- ¼ cup chopped onion

Place pheasant in a 13 x 9 x 2-inch baking pan, skin side up. Blend together soup, sour cream, mushrooms, cheese, and onion; spread over pheasant. Bake in preheated 350° oven 1½ to 2 hours or until pheasant is tender. Baste occasionally with sauce. Serves 4.

Pheasant

- 2 2-pound pheasants
- 2 tablespoons butter or margarine
- ½ teaspoon salt
- ¼ teaspoon pepper
- ½ cup diced celery
- ½ cup sliced onion
- ½ cup sliced carrots
- 2 slices salt pork
- 1 cup sliced mushrooms
- 2 cups chicken stock
- ½ cup Madeira wine
- 3 tablespoons flour
- 3 tablespoons butter or margarine, melted
  Wild Rice

Rub pheasant with about 2 tablespoons butter and sprinkle inside and out with salt and pepper. Stuff cavity with celery, onion and carrots. Place in roasting pan. Bake in a 400° oven for 20 minutes until brown. Reduce heat to 350°. Place salt pork over breast portions. Add mushrooms and chicken stock. Cover and roast about 40 minutes more until tender. Do not overcook, as the meat will become dry. When done, remove pheasant to a warm platter. Add wine. Thicken stock with 3 tablespoons melted butter mixed with 3 tablespoons flour. Simmer for 3 to 4 minutes. Pour sauce over pheasant and serve with Wild Rice. Serves 4.

Wild Rice

- 2 cups wild rice
- ½ cup minced onion
  Salt and pepper
- ½ cup minced celery
- ½ cup sliced mushrooms
- ¼ pound bacon, diced
- 1 tablespoon butter

Wash rice thoroughly several times. Place rice in a saucepan. Add hot water to cover, and boil for 5 minutes. Drain and rinse well. Cover again with hot water and boil another 35 minutes. Do not stir. Drain and rinse with cold water. Kernels should be flaky, not soft or mushy. Sauté bacon in butter until almost done. Add onion, celery, and mushrooms and cook for 5 minutes. Add wild rice and season with salt and pepper. Cook until rice is hot.

Marinade for Game Birds

- 4 onions, sliced
- 4 carrots, sliced
- 1 stalk celery, diced
- 2 bay leaves
- 12 peppercorns
- 1 clove garlic, crushed
- 1 quart wine

Mix all ingredients in a large bowl. Pour over game and refrigerate overnight. The wine and vegetables add a mellow flavor to the game. The marinade can be used to baste the game during cooking and then used for gravy.

Cornish Game Hens

Wash hens in cold water and dry. Brush skin with melted butter and sprinkle with seasoned salt. Place half a peeled orange in cavity. A stuffing may also be used, if desired. Place in baking pan. Add celery and onion around hens. Place in over 350° for 1 hour. Increase heat to 400° for last 10 minutes to brown. Add 1 cup chicken stock to pan drippings., and thicken with a smooth mixture of 2 tablespoons softened butter or margarine and 2 tablespoons flour.

Another way to prepare Cornish Game Hens is to split hens in half, brush with oil and sprinkle with salt and paprika. Place hens over a scoop of stuffing in a baking pan. Cover and bake for 1 hour at 350°. Make gravy from giblets and pour over hens the last 15 minutes.

Quail Julienne

- 8 quail
  Salt and pepper
  Butter or margarine
- ½ cup julienne carrots
- ½ cup julienne green onion
- ½ cup julienne celery
- ½ cup sliced mushrooms
- 3 tablespoons butter or margarine
- 3 tablespoons flour
- 2 cups chicken stock
- ½ cup orange juice
- ¼ cup orange peel, thinly sliced

Rub quail with butter, salt, and pepper. Brown in a 400 ° oven for 5 to 10 minutes. Sauté vegetables in 3 tablespoons butter for 5 minutes. Add flour and mix well. Stir in chicken stock, orange juice, and orange peel. Simmer for 1 to 2 minutes. Pour over quail, cover, and bake for 30 to 35 minutes in a 350° oven until tender. Serves 8.

Roast Partridge

- 4 partridges
  Salt and pepper, to taste
- 2 oranges
- ½ cup sliced onion
- ½ cup sliced celery
- ½ cup sliced carrots
- 4 slices bacon
- ½ cup butter, melted
- 1 cup chicken stock
- 3 tablespoons flour
- 3 tablespoons butter or margarine, melted
- 1 cup seedless grapes
- ½ cup toasted almonds

Rub partridges with salt and pepper inside and out. Peel oranges, cut in halves, and place one half in each partridge. Arrange onion, celery, and carrots in bottom of baking dish, then place partridges on top of vegetables. Lay one bacon slice on top of each partridge. Pour ½ cup butter over partridges. Cover and cook in a 350° oven for 30 minutes. Pour chicken stock over birds and bake for 15 minutes more until tender. Remove partridges and keep warm. Add flour mixed with melted butter to thicken drippings, and simmer for 3 to 4 minutes. Strain. Add grapes and almonds to sauce. Heat for 3 to 4 minutes. Serve with Vegetables and Brown Rice. Serves 4.

Vegetables and Brown Rice

- 4 tablespoons margarine
- ½ cup diced celery
- ½ cup diced onion
- ½ cup diced green pepper
- ¼ cup chopped parsley
- 4 cups cooked brown rice
- ½ cup diced olives
- 1 large tomato, diced
- 1½ teaspoons seasoned salt
- 1 cup shredded Cheddar cheese

In a large skillet, melt margarine. Sauté celery, onion, and pepper for 4 to 5 minutes. Add parsley, then brown rice. Mix well. Add olives, tomato, and seasoned salt. Cook 4 to 5 minutes more. Stir in cheese. Serves 4.

Cantonese Dishes

Chicken Chow Mein

- 1 pound raw chicken, thinly sliced
- 2 tablespoons vegetable oil
- 1 cup diced celery
- ½ cup sliced water chestnuts
- 1 cup sliced mushrooms
- 1 cup water or chicken stock
- 2 to 3 tablespoons soy sauce
- 1 cup bean sprouts
- ½ cup bamboo shoots
- ½ teaspoon salt
- 1 teaspoon sugar
- 1 teaspoon monosodium glutamate
- 2 tablespoons cornstarch mixed with 3 tablespoons water
- 4 cups chow mein noodles

In a large skillet, fry chicken in vegetable oil 4 to 5 minutes until almost done. Add celery and cook until tender, about 3 to 4 minutes. Add remaining ingredients, except cornstarch mixture and noodles. Bring to a boil. Stir in cornstarch mixture to thicken. Serve over chow mein noodles. Serves 4.

Chicken and Bean Sprout Chop Suey

- 1 pound raw chicken breasts, skinned, boned, and thinly sliced
- 1 clove garlic, diced
- 2 tablespoons vegetable oil
- 1 cup chicken stock
- 3 slices gingerroot
- ½ teaspoon salt
- ½ teaspoon sugar
- ½ teaspoon monosodium glutamate
- 1 tablespoon soy sauce
- 1 tablespoon cornstarch mixed with 2 tablespoons water
- 1 pound fresh bean sprouts
- 4 cups steamed rice

In a large frying pan, saute' chicken and garlic for 4 to 5 minutes in oil. Add chicken stock, gingerroot, salt, sugar, monosodium glutamate, and soy sauce. Thicken with cornstarch mixture. Add washed bean sprouts and cook 3 to 4 minutes. Serve over steamed rice. Serves 4.

Cantonese cooking methods are quick and easy and aid a busy cook in meal planning. Meats and vegetables retain more nutrients when prepared in this manner. Vegetables will always be crisp and colorful.

Chicken with Almonds

- 2 cups diced, raw chicken breasts
- ½ cup diced celery
- 3 tablespoons vegetable oil
- ½ cup diced water chestnuts
- ½ cup sliced mushrooms
- ½ cup diced bamboo shoots
- ½ teaspoon salt
- 1 teaspoon monosodium glutamate
- ½ teaspoon sugar
- 3 tablespoons soy sauce
- 1 cup water
- 1 cup sliced pea pods
- 2 tablespoons cornstarch mixed with 3 tablespoons water
- ¼ cup crushed toasted almonds

In a large skillet, saute' chicken and celery for 3 to 4 minutes in oil. Add water chestnuts, mushrooms, and bamboo shoots and cook for 1 to 2 minutes more. Mix in seasonings, sugar, soy sauce, and water. Add pea pods and cook 1 to 2 minutes more. Stir in cornstarch mixture and cook until thickened. Top with crushed toasted almonds. Serve with rice or chow mein noodles. Serves 4.

Chicken and Lobster Cantonese

- ¼ cup butter or margarine
- 2 cloves garlic, minced
- 2 cubed, cooked chicken breasts
- 2 5-ounce lobster tails, steamed or boiled, shelled and cut in ½-inch slices
- ½ cup sliced fresh mushrooms
- ½ cup thinly sliced bok-choi (Chinese cabbage)
- ½ cup sliced bamboo shoots
- 2 cups sliced water chestnuts
- 1 cup sliced pea pods
- 2½ cups chicken stock
- 1 teaspoon salt
- 1 teaspoon monosodium glutamate
- 1 teaspoon sugar
- 2 teaspoons soy sauce
- 3 tablespoons cornstarch mixed with 3 tablespoons water
- 6 cups cooked rice

Melt butter in a wok or large skillet. Add garlic, chicken, and lobster. Saute' 1 to 2 minutes. Add mushrooms, bok-choi, bamboo shoots, water chestnuts, and pea pods. Saute' for 2 to 3 minutes. Add remaining ingredients, except rice. Simmer for 3 to 4 minutes. Serve over rice. Serves 6.

Cantonese Dishes

Chicken Fried Rice

- 2 cups cooked rice
- 2 tablespoons vegetable oil
- 1 egg
- ½ cup diced mushrooms
- ½ cup diced water chestnuts
- ¼ cup chopped green onion tops
- 2 to 3 tablespoons soy sauce
- ½ cup bean sprouts
- 1 cup diced, cooked chicken
- ½ teaspoon monosodium glutamate

Fry rice in oil until warm. Add egg and scramble well. Stir in remaining ingredients and fry until brown. Serves 4.

Chinese Pressed Duck

- 1 4½- to 5-pound duck
- 4 cups water
- 1 teaspoon salt
- ½ teaspoon monosodium glutamate
- 3 tablespoons sugar
- 1 teaspoon Chinese cinnamon
- ½ cup soy sauce
- 3 tablespoons cornstarch mixed with ¼ cup water
- ½ cup water chestnut flour or powder
- ¼ cup water
  Oil
- ½ head lettuce
  Ground almonds for garnish

In a covered pot, simmer duck for 1 hour with the next 6 ingredients until tender. Remove duck and cool. Bring stock to a boil and thicken with cornstarch mixture. Correct seasoning and reserve to use as gravy. When duck is cool, place on platter, breast side down. Bone duck by cutting down backbone, being careful not to tear skin. Leave skin on platter. Remove all meat from bones and shred meat. Discard bones. Mix ½ cup water chestnut flour with shredded duck meat. Pack shredded meat mixture on ½ of duck skin. Press meat on tightly. Sprinkle with water. Cover with other ½ of duck skin and place duck and platter in steamer for 45 minutes. Remove from steamer and cool. When cool, remove from platter and cut in quarters. Place in refrigerator until ready to use. Deep fry duck in 350° oil for 5 minutes until brown. Cut duck in pieces. Shred lettuce and place on a serving platter. Add meat. Heat gravy and pour over duck. Garnish with ground almonds. Serves 4.

Chicken and Pineapple

- 3 cups Rice Pilaf (p. 57)
- 1 ripe pineapple
- 2 cooked and boned chicken breasts
- ½ cup brown sugar
- ¼ cup vinegar
- 1 cup water
  Pinch of salt
- 3 tablespoons butter or margarine
- 1½ tablespoons cornstarch mixed with 2 tablespoons water
- 2 cups Oriental vegetables

Prepare Rice Pilaf. Cut pineapple in half lengthwise. Hollow out pineapple and set pulp aside. Divide Rice Pilaf and spoon into pineapple. Place cooked chicken breasts on top of rice. Place in baking pan. Dice pineapple pulp and place in medium-size saucepan. Add brown sugar, vinegar, water, salt, and butter. Bring to a boil. Thicken with cornstarch mixture. Pour over chicken, wrap in foil and bake in a 350° oven for 30 to 40 minutes. Prepare Oriental vegetables just prior to serving. Serves 2.

Pineapple Chicken Flambe'

- 2 whole pineapples
- 2 cups pineapple juice
- 2 tablespoons butter
- 2 tablespoons cornstarch mixed with 2 tablespoons water
- 1 2½-pound fryer, cut in quarters
  Salt and paprika
- ¼ cup sherry
- ⅛ cup vegetable oil
- 2 cups cooked rice
- 1 ounce warm brandy

Cut whole pineapples in half lengthwise. Hollow out with a grapefruit knife. Cut core away from pulp and cut pineapple into bite-size pieces. Place pineapple in a large saucepan with pineapple juice. Add butter and bring to a boil. Thicken with cornstarch mixture. Simmer for 5 minutes. Brush chicken with sherry and cooking oil. Season with salt and paprika. Bake in a 350° oven for 45 minutes until brown. Remove from oven. When cool enough to handle, debone chicken. Place ½ cup of cooked rice in each pineapple shell. Divide chicken into four servings and place on rice. Divide sauce and pour over chicken. Cover each shell with aluminum foil. Bake in a 350° oven for 30 minutes. While still hot, remove foil and pour warm brandy over chicken. Ignite and serve.

Marinated Chicken

2½ pounds raw chicken, chopped
¼ cup soy sauce
¼ cup Sake or sherry
1 tablespoon sugar
½ cup cornstarch
½ cup vegetable oil

Marinate chicken in soy sauce, wine, and sugar for 1 hour. Remove chicken and roll in cornstarch. Let stand for 15 minutes. Fry in oil in a large skillet until brown and crispy. Serves 6.

Tahitian Rum Chicken

8 large chicken breasts
½ cup butter
 Salt and paprika
 Tahitian Sauce

Melt butter and brush over chicken breasts. Sprinkle with salt and paprika. Place in a large casserole and bake in a 375° oven for 20 minutes. Prepare Tahitian Sauce.

Tahitian Sauce

2 cups chicken stock
2 cups pineapple juice
½ cup catsup
½ cup white vinegar
¾ cup sugar
½ teaspoon salt
2 or 3 slices gingerroot
1½ tablespoons soy sauce
1 small clove garlic, minced
3 tablespoons cornstarch mixed with
 4 tablespoons water
2 medium carrots, thinly sliced
1 large green pepper, diced
2 cups pineapple chunks
8 cups cooked rice
3 ounces rum

In a large saucepan bring chicken stock, pineapple juice, catsup, vinegar, sugar, salt, gingerroot, soy sauce, and garlic to a boil. Stir in cornstarch mixture and simmer for 5 minutes. Add carrots, pepper, and pineapple. Stir well. Pour over chicken breasts in oven. Lower heat to 350° and bake 30 to 40 minutes more, or until done. Place chicken breasts over rice and add sauce. Warm rum and pour over chicken. Serves 8.

Note: This may be served in scooped out pineapple halves, using pineapple chunks for garnish.

Chicken Moo Goo Guy Pan

1 pound chicken breasts, boned and sliced
½ cup diced celery
1 cup sliced bok-choi (Chinese cabbage)
2 tablespoons peanut oil
½ cup sliced, dried black mushrooms, soaked in water
¼ cup sliced bamboo shoots
¼ cup sliced water chestnuts
1 cup sliced pea pods
1 cup chicken stock
½ teaspoon salt
½ teaspoon monosodium glutamate
½ teaspoon sugar
1 tablespoon soy sauce
1 tablespoon cornstarch mixed with
 2 tablespoons water

In a large skillet saute' chicken, celery, and bok-choi in oil for 7 to 8 minutes. Add black mushrooms, bamboo shoots, chestnuts, and pea pods. Stir in chicken stock, salt, monosodium glutamate, sugar, soy sauce, and cornstarch mixture. Simmer for 6 to 7 minutes. Serve with steamed rice. Serves 4.

Egg Foo Yung

6 eggs
1 cup cooked chicken
1 4-ounce can bamboo shoots, diced
1 4-ounce can water chestnuts, diced
1 4-ounce can mushrooms, sliced
1 pound fresh or canned bean sprouts
1 teaspoon soy sauce
½ teaspoon salt
½ teaspoon sugar
½ teaspoon monosodium glutamate
 Vegetable oil
 Egg Foo Yung Gravy

Beat eggs. Add remaining ingredients, except oil, and mix well. Heat 2 inches of oil in a heavy, deep pan. Spoon or ladle ¼ of egg mixture in pan and brown for 2 minutes. Baste top of omelet with hot oil and flip. Cook on other side for 1½ minutes. Remove and drain. Repeat with rest of mixture. Serve with Egg Foo Yung Gravy. Serves 4.

Egg Foo Yung Gravy

1 cup chicken stock
½ teaspoon sugar
1 teaspoon monosodium glutamate
¼ cup soy sauce
1½ teaspoons cornstarch mixed with 1 tablespoon water

Bring chicken stock to a boil in a small saucepan. Add all other ingredients. Simmer for 2 minutes. Serve over Egg Foo Yung.

Eggs

Eggs Benedict

    8 eggs
    4 English muffins
    8 small slices of ham or Canadian bacon
      Hollandaise Sauce

Poach eggs. Split and toast muffins. Layer ham, then eggs over muffins. Top with Hollandaise Sauce. Serves 4.

Hollandaise Sauce

    4 egg yolks
1½ tablespoons lukewarm water
    1 cup melted, clarified butter
      Juice from half a lemon
      Dash cayenne pepper
      Dash salt

Set an earthenware bowl in a pan of hot water. In bowl, combine egg yolks with lukewarm water. Stir briskly with a wire whip until mixture thickens slightly, about 2 to 3 minutes. Pour butter in very slowly and continue to beat sauce until fluffy and thick. Remove bowl from water and add lemon juice and seasoning. If sauce shows signs of curdling, add a little hot water or 2 tablespoons cream, beating constantly to thicken. Makes 1 cup.

Creamed Eggs and Broccoli

    3 tablespoons butter or margarine
    3 tablespoons flour
    1 cup chicken bouillon
    1 cup milk
    1 teaspoon seasoned salt
    8 hard-boiled eggs, shelled and sliced
    6 English muffins, split
   12 stalks cooked broccoli or asparagus
      Parmesan cheese
      Paprika

Melt butter. Add flour and simmer for one minute. Add chicken bouillon, then milk and seasoned salt. Cook until thickened. Add eggs and simmer for 3 to 4 minutes. Place English muffins on baking sheet, then place broccoli on each English muffin half. Pour egg mixture over muffins. Sprinkle with Parmesan cheese and paprika. Bake in a 375° oven for 10 to 12 minutes. Serves 6.

Beat egg whites in a copper bowl with a whisk to achieve the most volume possible.

Eggs Mornay

    1 pound bulk pork sausage
    2 tablespoons flour
2½ cups milk
    1 cup shredded cheese (4 ounces)
    1 teaspoon seasoned salt
    4 English muffins, split
    8 eggs, poached
      Chopped parsley

Form sausage into 8 patties and pan fry. When done, remove from pan and keep warm. Add flour to 3 tablespoons pork drippings. Stir and simmer for 1 minute. Slowly stir in milk and allow to thicken. Add cheese and seasoned salt and mix well. Toast muffins and place one pork patty on each muffin. Add one poached egg to each. Pour sauce over eggs and sprinkle with chopped parsley. Serves 4.

Deviled Eggs

   12 hard-boiled eggs, shelled and cut in half
    2 tablespoons mustard
    2 tablespoons butter or margarine, softened
   ½ cup mayonnaise
   ½ teaspoon salt
   ¼ teaspoon pepper
      Dash of Tabasco sauce
      Paprika

Remove egg yolks and mash with remaining ingredients, except paprika, until smooth. Spoon mixture into egg halves or place in a pastry bag with a star tube and squeeze into egg halves. Sprinkle with paprika. Makes 24.

Deviled Eggs
Egg Salad, page 41

Eggs

Omelets

Select filling for omelet, such as 1 large slice Cheddar or Swiss cheese, shredded, ¼ cup diced cooked ham, or 2 tablespoons strawberry preserves, or sautéed mushrooms. Break 2 eggs into a bowl and beat thoroughly. Season with salt and white pepper to taste. Melt 1 tablespoon butter in an omelet pan or 7-inch skillet over medium heat. Pour eggs into pan. As eggs thicken, carefully pull back edges and tip pan so uncooked egg flows underneath. When omelet is set, place filling over ½ of omelet and fold other ½ over. Slide omelet onto a warm platter.

Baked Egg Omelet

½ cup diced onion
½ cup diced green pepper
1 cup diced mushrooms
1 tomato, diced
½ cup butter or margarine
8 eggs, beaten
2 cups milk
1 cup shredded Cheddar cheese
2 teaspoons seasoned salt

Sauté onion, pepper, mushrooms, and tomato in butter for 4 to 5 minutes. Cool. Mix with eggs. Add milk, cheese, and seasoned salt. Pour into greased baking dish. Bake in a 350° oven for 30 to 35 minutes or until firm. Serves 6 to 8.

Variation: add 1 cup diced spinach, cooked and drained, to above ingredients.

Potato Omelet

¼ pound bacon, ham, or sausage, diced
2 tablespoons butter
½ cup diced onion
½ cup diced celery
2 potatoes, boiled and diced
8 eggs
½ cup milk or light cream
Salt and pepper
Chopped parsley

In a large skillet, sauté bacon, ham, or sausage in butter. Add onion, celery, and potatoes. Cook until light brown. Beat eggs with milk. Add salt and pepper. Pour over meat and vegetable mixture. Add parsley and cover. Cook until eggs are set, about 4 to 5 minutes. Serve hot on a warm platter. Serves 6.

Save small portions of leftover sauce, such as Piquant Tomato Sauce or Creole Sauce. Warm thoroughly and serve with omelets.

Puffy Omelet

½ teaspoon salt
¼ cup water
4 eggs, separated
Dash white pepper or Tabasco sauce
1 tablespoon butter

Add salt and water to egg whites. Beat until stiff and shiny and whites leave peaks when beater is taken out. Add pepper to yolks; beat until thick and lemon colored. Fold yolks into egg whites. Heat butter in 10-inch oven proof skillet until just hot enough to sizzle a drop of water. Pour in omelet mixture. Reduce heat. Level surface gently. Cook slowly until puffy and lightly browned on bottom, about 5 minutes. Lift omelet gently at edge to judge color. Place in preheated 325° oven. Bake until knife inserted in center comes out clean, 12 to 15 minutes. To serve: tear gently, using 2 forks, into individual servings. Invert pieces on serving plate so browned bottom becomes the top. If you like, omelet may be folded in half. Serves 2.

Basic Crepes

3 tablespoons butter
3 eggs, slightly beaten
½ cup milk
½ cup water
¾ cup all-purpose flour
⅛ teaspoon salt
Butter

Melt butter in 8-inch crepe or omelet pan. In mixing bowl, combine eggs, milk, water and melted butter; beat with rotary beater. Blend in flour and salt until mixture is smooth. Refrigerate batter 2 hours or overnight. Place buttered crepe pan over medium-high heat until hot enough to sizzle a drop of water. For each crepe pour 3 tablespoons or scant ¼ cup batter in pan, rotating pan as batter is poured. Crepes should set a thin lacy pancake almost immediately. If too much batter is poured into pan, pour off excess immediately. If there are holes, add a drop or two of batter for a patch. Cook until lightly browned on bottom; turn and brown other side. It may be necessary to add more butter to grease pan before pouring in batter for each crepe. Stack crepes between sheets of paper toweling or waxed paper until ready to use. May be prepared in advance and frozen between sheets of waxed paper. Yield: 12 to 14 crepes.

Cheese Soufflé

Butter
Grated Parmesan cheese
2 tablespoons butter
4 tablespoons flour
1 cup light cream, cold
½ teaspoon salt
⅛ teaspoon nutmeg
⅛ teaspoon white pepper
5 jumbo egg yolks
½ cup grated Parmesan cheese
6 jumbo egg whites, room temperature
¼ teaspoon cream of tartar
3 drops yellow food coloring
1 drop red food coloring

Grease a 6-cup soufflé dish well with butter. Sprinkle with grated Parmesan cheese. Melt 2 tablespoons butter in saucepan; stir in flour. Cook a few minutes. (Do not brown flour.) Stir in cold light cream. Add salt, nutmeg, and pepper, cooking until thick. Remove from heat. Beat egg yolks with wire whisk; stir some of hot sauce into beaten yolks. Mix well and stir yolks into sauce. Add cheese and mix. Cover until you complete the remaining steps for the soufflé. Soufflé can be prepared up to this point several hours ahead of baking time.

Preheat oven to 350°. If previous mixture was made ahead, heat over low heat. As it heats, start by stirring in the center and gradually work your way to the sides of the pan, blending gently. Heat only to lukewarm and then remove from heat. Beat egg whites with cream of tartar in a bowl until stiff but not dry. Do not overbeat or whites will loose volume. Use a rubber spatula and keep whites pushed away from the sides into the center. When the large bubbles disappear, add the food coloring and beat until stiff. (Color whites to match yolk mixture, otherwise they dilute the yellow color of the soufflé. Uncolored whites show up as white patches.) With a wire whisk, stir about 1 cup of the whites into the yolk mixture. Use a rubber spatula to fold in the remaining whites. Pour into prepared soufflé dish. Bake in preheated 350° oven 40 to 45 minutes. Serve immediately as is or with Creole Sauce, (p. 8).

Use leftover chicken or turkey and vegetables in a White Sauce or Cheese Sauce as a main dish filling for crepes. Add a crunchy taste with peanuts or sliced water chestnuts.

Egg Salad

6 hard-boiled eggs, shelled and chopped
¼ cup pickle relish
¼ cup diced, stuffed olives
½ cup mayonnaise
¼ teaspoon salt
⅛ teaspoon pepper
2 slices bacon, diced, optional

Combine all ingredients. Add two slices of crisp, diced bacon for extra flavor, if desired. Chill. Use for sandwich filling or salad.

Egg and Chicken Spread

4 hard-boiled eggs, shelled and minced
1 cup minced, cooked chicken
½ cup pickle relish
½ cup chopped celery
½ cup mayonnaise
Salt and pepper to taste

Mix all together and chill until ready to use. Makes 3 cups.

German Apple Pancake

6 eggs, separated
¼ cup flour
¼ cup butter, melted
¼ cup milk
½ teaspoon salt
2 tablespoons butter
3 apples, sliced
Sugar
Cinnamon

Beat egg yolks; mix in flour, butter, milk, and salt. Beat egg whites and fold in. Heat 2 tablespoons butter in a large skillet; pour in batter. Top with apple slices. Cook over medium heat for about 5 minutes. Bake in a 400° oven for 15 minutes until golden brown. Top with sugar and cinnamon. Serves 2 to 4.

Sherried Eggs and Cheddar Cheese

8 eggs
6 tablespoons sherry
Salt and pepper
2 tablespoons butter
1 cup grated Cheddar cheese
8 slices buttered toast

Beat eggs and sherry until light. Add salt and pepper. Melt butter in frying pan. When butter is hot, pour in eggs. Stir until smooth. Add Cheddar cheese and stir until cheese melts. When set, serve on hot, buttered toast. Serves 4.

Scrambled Eggs and Hot Dogs

3 tablespoons butter
8 hot dogs, cut in ¼-inch slices
½ cup diced onion
½ cup sliced green pepepr
½ cup diced salad olives
2 medium tomatoes, diced
½ cup milk
1 teaspoon seasoned salt
8 eggs
6 to 8 English muffins
1 cup shredded Cheddar cheese, optional

Melt butter in a large skillet. Add hot dogs, onion, and pepper. Saute' for 3 to 4 minutes. Add olives and tomatoes. Mix well. Cook 2 minutes more. Beat eggs with milk and add seasoned salt. Add to skillet mixture. Cook several minutes until thickened. Serve over muffins. Sprinkle with cheese, if desired. Serves 6 to 8.

Scrambled Eggs, Tomatoes, and Chives

2 fresh tomatoes, diced
2 tablespoons chives
3 tablespoons butter
8 eggs, beaten
¼ teaspoon salt
½ cup light cream
Parsley

Saute' tomatoes and chives in butter. Add eggs, salt, and cream. Stir over low heat until eggs are almost set. Serve on a hot platter and garnish with parsley. Serves 4.

Note: For a different taste, add 2½ cups diced chicken and ¼ teaspoon curry powder. Serves 4 to 6.

Quiche Lorraine

2 cups thinly sliced onion
3 tablespoons butter
1 cup sour cream
2 eggs, slightly beaten
1 teaspoon salt
¼ teaspoon pepper
Pinch of ginger
¼ teaspoon nutmeg
2 tablespoons caraway seed
½ pound bacon, diced, fried, and drained
Paprika

Make Cream Cheese Pastry and line quiche or pie pan or 12 individual tins. Saute' onion in butter until golden; add remaining ingredients. Pour into crust. Sprinkle with paprika. Bake at 450° for 10 minutes. Reduce heat to 350° and bake 30 minutes longer, or until knife inserted into custard comes out clean.

Cream Cheese Pastry

¾ cup flour
¼ teaspoon salt
4 ounces cream cheese, softened
½ cup butter, softened

Stir salt into flour. Cut in cream cheese and butter. Roll out on lightly floured surface.

Easy Scrambled Eggs

4 eggs
4 tablespoons milk or light cream
⅛ teaspoon salt
2 tablespoons butter or margarine

Beat eggs. Add milk and salt. Melt butter in a frying pan over medium heat. Pour in eggs. When eggs start to thicken, stir with a wooden spoon. Remove from heat while they are soft. They will finish cooking from the heat retained in the frying pan. Serves 2.

Scrambled Eggs Cooked in the Oven

12 eggs
4 cups milk
2 teaspoons seasoned salt
1 cup margarine, melted

Beat together eggs, milk, seasoned salt, and melted margarine. Pour into a greased baking dish. Bake in a 350° oven for 20 to 25 minutes, stirring frequently. Serves 8.

Note: Any cooked meat, vegetable, or mushrooms may be added before baking.

Easy Scrambled Eggs

Soups and Sandwiches

Chicken Broth

    4 to 5-pound stewing chicken, cut up
1¼ quarts hot water
    2 teaspoons salt
       Dash Pepper
    5 3-inch pieces of celery with leaves
    3 small carrots
    2 medium onions

Place chicken, reserving liver, in large stockpot. Add water, salt, pepper, and vegetables. Cover and bring to a boil. Reduce heat. Uncover and remove foam. Simmer covered 2 to 3 hours, adding the liver for the last 15 minutes. Remove chicken from broth. Strain the broth through a cheesecloth-lined colander. Cool slightly. Skim off the fat that rises to the top. Refrigerate until needed. Yield: about 1 quart.

Greek Egg and Lemon Soup

    8 cups chicken broth
    3 tablespoons butter
1⅓ cups long grain white rice
    1 teaspoon salt
   ⅛ teaspoon white pepper
    3 eggs
       Juice of 1½ large lemons
       Chopped parsley

In a large saucepan, bring chicken broth and butter to boil over high heat. Stir rice, salt, and pepper into hot broth; bring to a boil. Reduce heat to simmer; cook until rice is tender. With electric mixer, beat eggs until thick and light-colored, about 7 to 10 minutes; or process in blender on high speed . Add lemon juice to eggs, beating constantly. Pour in broth, a little at a time beating until most of broth is used. Slowly pour this mixture back into the saucepan, stirring constantly. Sprinkle parsley over top of hot soup. Serve at once. Serves 8.

Chinese Egg Drop Soup

    4 cups chicken broth
    2 eggs, lightly beaten
    2 tablespoons parsley, chopped

Bring chicken broth to a boil. Whisk broth slowly, pouring the beaten egg into the hot broth so that it cooks in threads. Serve immediately. Sprinkle with parsley. Serves 4 to 6.

Cream of Chicken Vegetable Soup

    1 cup diced celery
    1 cup diced onion
    4 tablespoons margarine
    4 cups chicken stock
    3 tablespoons flour
    2 cups milk or light cream
    2 cups cooked vegetable (broccoli, spinach,
       lima beans, zucchini, squash, corn, or cucumbers)
    2 teaspoons seasoned salt
    1 cup cooked, diced chicken

Saute' celery and onion in 1 tablespoon margarine in a skillet for 4 minutes. Add to chicken stock in a saucepan and simmer for 20 minutes. Mix remaining margarine with flour in skillet and cook for 1 to 2 minutes. Add to chicken stock and mix well. Simmer stock for 5 minutes more. Stir in milk, then cooked vegetable and chicken. Add seasoning and simmer 4 to 5 minutes.

Note: One cup cooked potatoes, macaroni, or rice can be added, if desired. Serves 6 to 8.

Chicken Noodle Soup

    3 pounds fryer backs
    2 quarts water
    1 teaspoon salt
    1 cup diced carrots
    1 cup diced celery
    1 cup diced onion
   ¼ pound margarine
   ½ cup mushrooms, optional
    3 tablespoons chopped parsley
   ½ teaspoon Worcestershire sauce
       Dash Tabasco sauce
    1 pound broad noodles, cooked

Bring backs to a boil in salted water and simmer for 1 hour. Strain, and save stock for soup. Remove any meat from bones and add to stock. Saute' carrots, celery, and onion in margarine for 5 minutes. Add vegetables, mushrooms, sauces, and parsley to stock and simmer until vegetables are tender, about 25 to 30 minutes. Cook noodles separately. Rinse and drain noodles and add to chicken stock. Bring to a boil and serve. Serves 8 to 10.

Freeze stock in 1-cup portions. Then thaw as needed for recipes using stock. May be added frozen to soups for extra flavor.

Chicken and Yellow Split Pea Soup

- 2 cups yellow split peas
- 12 cups chicken stock
- ½ cup diced bacon
- 1 cup diced carrots
- 1 cup diced onion
- 2 cups diced, cooked chicken
- 2 teaspoons salt
- ¼ teaspoon pepper
- Croutons

Soak split peas in water overnight. Drain, sort and simmer in chicken stock in a large saucepan until tender. When tender, mash peas or force through strainer. Return strained peas to stock. Sauté bacon and vegetables for 5 minutes over medium heat. Add to chicken stock and peas. Stir in diced chicken and seasonings. Simmer until vegetables are tender, about 25 to 30 minutes. Serve hot with croutons. Serves 6 to 8.

Cabbage Soup

- 1 large onion, sliced
- 2 tablespoons olive oil or butter
- 1 small head cabbage, shredded
- 8 cups chicken stock
- 4 potatoes, peeled and diced
- ¼ teaspoon crushed garlic
- 3 bay leaves
- 1½ teaspoons salt
- ¼ teaspoon white pepper
- 1 tablespoons sugar
- 4 chicken hot dogs, sliced

In a large skillet, sauté onion in oil until golden. Add cabbage, mix with onion and cook for 2 to 3 minutes. Stir in chicken stock and potatoes. Add garlic, bay leaves, salt, and white pepper. Cook until tender. Remove bay leaves. Add sugar, hot dogs, and heat thoroughly. Serves 6 to 8.

Chicken Swiss Sandwich Puff

- 2 cups diced, cooked chicken
- 1 cup shredded Swiss cheese
- ½ cup chopped, stuffed green olives
- ½ cup diced celery
- 2 eggs, well beaten
- ¾ cup mayonnaise
- 1 teaspoon seasoned salt
- 4 English muffins, split
- Paprika
- Parsley

Combine first seven ingredients. Spread mixture on muffin halves. Sprinkle with parsley and paprika. Bake in a 350° oven for 15 minutes. Serves 8.

Turkey Soup

- Turkey Stock
- 2 cups diced celery
- 2 cups chopped onion
- 2 cups chopped carrots
- ½ cup butter or margarine
- 2 cups noodles, cooked
- Leftover turkey, diced
- Dash of Tabasco sauce
- 1 teaspoon Worcestershire sauce
- 1 tablespoon chicken base or bouillon
- 2 tablespoons chopped parsley
- Salt and pepper to taste

To make turkey stock, cover leftover turkey bones with water and simmer 1½ hours. Strain and reserve. Remove turkey from bones and dice meat. Sauté celery, onion, and carrots in butter for 5 minutes until golden. Add enough water to turkey stock to make 2 quarts. Stir in sautéed mixture and simmer until tender, about 20 minutes. Mix in noodles and diced turkey. Simmer 10 minutes more. Add remaining ingredients.

Italian Chicken Sandwich

- 2 cups cubed, cooked chicken
- 1 small onion, diced
- 1 green pepper, chopped
- 1 clove garlic, diced
- ¼ cup margarine or olive oil
- 1 4-ounce can mushrooms or 1 cup fresh mushrooms, sliced
- 4 cups medium tomatoes, diced
- 1 cup sliced, pitted, black olives
- 1 teaspoon seasoned salt
- 1 loaf French bread
- ½ cup Parmesan cheese

In a large skillet, sauté chicken, onion, pepper, and garlic in margarine for 5 minutes. Add mushrooms, tomatoes, olives, and seasoned salt. Cut French bread lengthwise and place on baking sheet. Spread chicken and vegetables over bread and sprinkle with Parmesan cheese. Bake in a 350° oven for 8 to 10 minutes. Cut French bread into serving pieces after baking.

Note: Mixture may be spread on individual rolls. Serves 6 to 8.

Fried Egg Burger

1 pound ground beef
1 tablespoon chopped green pepper
1 tablespoon chopped parsley
1 tablespoon chopped onion
3 tablespoons bread crumbs
1 teaspoon seasoned salt
1 egg
3 English muffins, split
6 poached eggs
   Cheese Sauce (p. 61)

Mix ground beef, green pepper, parsley, onion, bread crumbs, seasoning, and egg together. Shape into six patties and pan fry. Layer patties, then poached eggs over English muffins. Top with Cheese Sauce. Serves 6.

Chicken Taco Burger

2 cups chopped, cooked chicken
3 tablespoons butter or margarine
¼ teaspoon garlic powder
¼ teaspoon cumin
½ teaspoon salt
¼ teaspoon chili powder
1 8-ounce can tomato sauce
1 16-ounce can tomatoes
6 toasted hamburger buns, sliced and toasted
   Shredded lettuce, cheese, and chopped onion

In a medium-size skillet, brown chicken in butter. Add spices, tomato sauce, and tomatoes. Simmer for 15 minutes and spoon over toasted buns. Garnish with shredded lettuce, cheese, and chopped onion. Serves 6.

Clubhouse Sandwich

3 slices of bread, toasted
2 slices cooked turkey or chicken white meat
1 lettuce leaf
2 tablespoons mayonnaise
2 slices bacon, fried and drained
2 slices tomato

Butter toast. Cover one slice of toast with turkey slices and lettuce leaf, then place another slice of toast with mayonnaise on top. Add bacon and tomato and cover with last piece of toast. Fasten securely with toothpicks. Cut sandwich diagonally into four triangles and stand them upright. Serve with olives, pickles, and potato salad, if desired. Makes 1 sandwich.

Deep-Fried Pineapple and Chicken Sandwich

1 cup chopped, cooked chicken
½ cup crushed pineapple, drained
½ cup mayonnaise
8 slices white or raisin bread
2 eggs
2 cups vegetable oil
   Confectioners' sugar
   Jelly

Mix chicken, pineapple, and mayonnaise together. Spread on 4 slices of bread, cover with remaining 4 slices of bread, and trim crusts. Cut each sandwich in three parts. Beat eggs and dip sandwiches in beaten egg. Fry sandwiches in 350° oil in a deep fryer until brown. Drain on absorbent paper. Garnish with confectioners' sugar and serve with jelly. Serves 4.

Chicken Cheese Sandwich

½ cup margarine
2 cups cooked, shredded chicken
1 medium onion, sliced
1 green pepper, julienne sliced
2 stalks celery, julienne sliced
1 cucumber, sliced
½ cup chicken stock
2 tomatoes, chopped
1½ teaspoons seasoned salt
1 tablespoon cornstarch mixed with
   1 tablespoon water
1 cup ricotta or other cheese, crumbled
6 whole-grain rolls or large buns

Melt margarine in skillet and add chicken, onion, pepper, celery, and cucumber. Sauté for 5 minutes, then add chicken stock and tomatoes. Heat through, then add seasoned salt and cornstarch mixture. Simmer for 2 minutes. Add cheese, mix quickly, and spoon over heated rolls or buns. Serves 6.

Salads and Dressings

Rice Salad

- 4 cups cooked rice
- ½ cup yogurt or sour cream
- ½ cup mayonnaise
- ¼ cup cooked peas
- ½ cup diced celery
- ¼ cup diced green salad olives
- 1 teaspoon seasoned salt
- 1 cup chopped, cooked chicken
- Hard-boiled eggs, shelled and sliced
- Tomatoes, cut in wedges
- Lettuce

Mix all ingredients together except eggs, tomatoes, and lettuce. Gently press rice mixture into a large mold and unmold on a bed of lettuce. Garnish with hard-boiled egg slices and tomato, if desired. Serves 6 to 8.

Pineapple Delight

Cut pineapple in quarters lengthwise, leaving leaves on. Cut out pineapple pulp and remove core. Slice pineapple in quarter-inch pieces and place back in pineapple shell, alternating with grapefruit, avocado, and shrimp. Serve with Old-Fashioned French Dressing (p. 54).

Party Time Tossed Salad

- 1 avocado, diced
- Lemon juice
- 1 small head romaine lettuce
- 1 head iceburg lettuce
- ½ cup salad shrimp, diced
- 2 tomatoes, cut in eighths
- 2 hard-boiled eggs, shelled and sliced
- ¼ cup blue cheese
- 1 teaspoon Worcestershire sauce
- Dash of garlic powder
- ½ teaspoon salt
- ¼ teaspoon pepper
- ¾ cup vegetable oil
- ⅛ cup wine vinegar
- Juice from 1 lemon
- Parmesan cheese

Sprinkle avocado with lemon juice to prevent it from turning dark. Tear romaine and iceburg lettuce in bite-size pieces. Wash, drain, and chill lettuce. Mix shrimp, tomatoes, hard-boiled eggs, blue cheese, Worcestershire sauce, garlic powder, salt, and pepper. Toss together. Add oil, wine vinegar, lemon juice, and lettuce. Mix well. Sprinkle with Parmesan cheese. Serve on chilled plates. Serves 6 to 8.

Cole Slaw

- 1 small head cabbage, shredded
- 2 red apples, diced
- 1 green pepper, diced
- ½ cup chopped dill pickle
- 2 large carrots, shredded
- ¼ cup pimiento, diced

Mix all ingredients together well. Toss with Creamy Dressing or Oil and Vinegar Dressing.

Creamy Dressing

- 1½ cups mayonnaise
- ¼ cup lemon juice
- ¼ cup sugar
- 1 cup sour cream
- ⅛ cup buttermilk
- 1 teaspoon seasoned salt

Mix ingredients together well. Pour dressing over other ingredients and toss. Chill. Serves 8.

Oil and Vinegar Dressing

- 1 cup vegetable oil
- ½ cup cider vinegar
- ½ cup sugar
- 1 teaspoon seasoned salt.

Combine all ingredients.

Carrot and Raisin Salad

- ¾ cup raisins
- 3 cups grated carrots
- ½ cup mayonnaise
- ¼ cup sour cream
- ½ teaspoon salt
- 2 tablespoons sugar
- 1 teaspoon lemon juice
- Lettuce leaves
- ½ cup chopped walnuts, optional
- ½ cup diced pineapple, optional

Pour raisins into 1½ cups boiling water, reduce heat and simmer 4 to 5 minutes. Drain and let cool. Mix carrots and raisins with mayonnaise and sour cream. Gently mix in salt, sugar, and lemon juice. Serve on crisp lettuce leaves. Walnuts and diced pineapple add extra flavor. Serves 4 to 6.

Wash, dry, and tear enough salad greens for two meals at once. Store ½ in an airtight plastic bag, without dressing, for the next meal.

Cucumber Salad

- ¼ cup sugar
- ½ cup vinegar
- 1 cup water
- ¼ cup vegetable oil
- 2 cucumbers, peeled and sliced
- 1 green pepper, diced
- 1 tomato, cut in eighths
- 1 onion, sliced
- Salt and pepper to taste
- 2 cooked knackwurst, sliced, optional

Mix sugar, vinegar, water, and oil together. Pour over cucumber, pepper, tomato, and onion. Mix well. Season to taste. Add 2 cooked sliced knackwurst, if desired. Serves 4.

Holiday Salad

- 2 cups diced apples
- Lemon juice
- 1 cup diced Cheddar cheese
- 1 cup mandarin oranges, drained
- 1 cup diced, cooked chicken
- ½ cup walnuts
- ½ cup diced celery
- 1 cup mayonnaise
- ¼ cup Old-Fashioned French Dressing (p. 54)
- Lettuce
- Whipped cream or yogurt

Sprinkle apples with lemon juice to prevent them from turning dark. Combine all ingredients with French Dressing and mayonnaise. Chill well. Serve on lettuce leaf and decorate with whipped cream or yogurt. Serves 6.

Fire and Ice Tomatoes

- 6 large tomatoes
- ¼ cup finely chopped onion
- 2 teaspoons basil
- Salt to taste
- ¼ cup wine vinegar
- ¾ cup olive oil
- 1 clove garlic, finely chopped
- 1 teaspoon Worcestershire sauce
- ½ teaspoon black pepper
- ½ teaspoon sugar

Thickly slice tomatoes and arrange one layer in serving bowl. Mix onion, basil, and some salt to taste together. Sprinkle some of this mixture on the tomatoes; continue to layer tomatoes and sprinkle onion mixture until all tomatoes are used. In a jar, combine wine vinegar, olive oil, garlic, Worcestershire sauce, pepper, and sugar. Pour over the tomatoes and chill well.

Health Fruit Salad

- 2 cups diced, fresh pineapple
- 2 apples, diced and sprinkled with lemon juice
- 2 oranges, peeled and sliced
- 2 bananas, sliced and sprinkled with lemon juice
- 1 cup fruit, any kind in sesaon
- ½ cup grated carrots
- ½ cup walnuts
- ⅓ cup honey
- 1 cup yogurt

Mix all ingredients together gently and chill. Serve in an elegant glass compote. Serves 8.

Cucumbers in Sour Cream

- 3 medium cucumbers, thinly sliced
- 3 cups water
- 1½ teaspoons salt
- ½ cup sour cream
- 2 tablespoons cider vinegar
- 1 teaspoon sugar
- ½ teaspoon salt
- ½ teaspoon black pepper

Layer cucumbers in a medium-size bowl. Cover with water and 1½ teaspoons salt. Chill. Pour off salted water and rinse. Drain. Blend sour cream, vinegar, and sugar. Fold into cucumbers. Sprinkle with salt and pepper.

Seven Layer Salad

- 1 head lettuce, shredded
- ½ cup chopped celery
- ½ cup chopped green onion
- ½ cup diced green pepper
- 1 10-ounce box frozen peas, cooked and drained
- 1 pint mayonnaise
- 2 tablespoons sugar
- 8 strips bacon, cooked, drained, and crumbled
- ½ cup grated Cheddar cheese

In a large glass bowl, place lettuce, then layers of celery, onion, pepper, and peas. Spread mayonnaise to the edges of the bowl, sealing all. Sprinkle with sugar, then layer with bacon and cheese. Cover tightly with plastic wrap and refrigerate until serving. May be prepared a day ahead.

Salads and Dressings

Cranberry Relish Salad

- 2 3-ounce packages raspberry gelatin
- 1 15-ounce can whole cranberry relish
- 1 cup diced celery
- ½ cup chopped walnuts
- 1 8½-ounce can crushed pineapple, drained, reserve juice

Dissolve gelatin in 2 cups boiling water. Stir in juice from pineapple. Add all other ingredients and mix well. Pour into large mold. Chill until firm. Serves 8 to 10.

Chicken Salad

- 2 cups cubed, cooked chicken
- 1½ cups diced celery
- ¼ cup diced onion
- 1 tablespoon lemon juice
- 1 teaspoon salt
- ¼ teaspoon pepper
- 1 tablespoon Worcestershire sauce
- 1 cup mayonnaise
- Lettuce leaves
- Hard-boiled eggs, shelled and sliced
- Olives
- Tomato wedges

Mix all ingredients together and chill well. Place on lettuce leaf and shredded lettuce. Garnish with hard-boiled egg slices, olives, and tomato. Serves 4.

Chicken Fruit Salad

- 2 cups cubed, cooked chicken
- 1 cup diced apples
- ½ cup diced green pepepr
- ½ cup diced celery
- ¾ cup mayonnaise
- 1 teaspoon lemon juice
- ⅛ teaspoon salt
- ¼ cup pecans, almonds, or walnuts
- Lettuce leaves
- Pear halves, drained
- Cream cheese, softened
- Red grapes, halved and seeded

Mix all ingredients together except lettuce, pears, cream cheese, and grapes, Mold in cups and serve on lettuce leaves. To make a garnish with drained pears, place pears cut-side down and spread with cream cheese. Press halved grapes into cheese, placing grapes close together to make pears look like bunches of grapes. Place next to salad. Serves 4.

Poach leftover egg yolks until firm. Cook and press through a sieve. Use in egg spread or to garnish a salad.

Greek Country Salad

- 1 large head iceberg lettuce
- 2 cups cherry tomatoes, sliced
- 1 large cucumber, sliced
- 1 cup sliced radishes
- 8 ounces Feta cheese, crumbled
- 2 4-ounce cans skinless, boneless sardines, drained
- ½ cup pitted ripe olives, halved
- ½ cup chopped green onions
- ¼ cup chopped parsley
- ⅓ cup olive or vegetable oil
- 3 tablespoons lemon juice
- ½ teaspoon oregano
- ½ teaspoon salt
- ⅛ teaspoon pepper

Line a large shallow bowl with lettuce leaves. Break the remainder of the lettuce into bite-size pieces and place in the bowl. Arrange tomatoes, cucumbers, radishes, cheese, sardines, olives, and green onions over the lettuce. Sprinkle with parsley. Combine oil, lemon juice, oregano, salt, and pepper in a jar and shake well to mix. Toss salad lightly with dressing before serving.

Hot Bacon Salad

- 6 slices bacon, diced
- 1 medium onion, minced
- ⅓ cup cider vinegar
- 3 tablespoons sugar
- 1½ teaspoons salt
- ¼ teaspoon pepper
- ¼ teaspoon dry mustard
- 2 eggs, slightly beaten
- 2 heads Boston lettuce
- 1 10-ounce bag spinach

Tear lettuce and spinach in bite-size pieces and place in bowl. In a medium skillet, fry bacon over medium heat until brown. Drain on paper towel. In bacon drippings, sauté onion until tender. Add vinegar, sugar, salt, pepper, and mustard. Cook until sugar dissolves. Add a small amount of hot mixture to beaten eggs. Slowly pour eggs back into remaining onion mixture. Cook, but do not boil, and stir rapidly to prevent lumping. When thickened, pour hot mixture over salad greens. Toss well. Serve immediately.

Chicken Fruit Salad

Salads and Dressings

Marinated Salad

- 1 tablespoon vegetable oil
- 1 teaspoon salt
- 1/3 cup granulated sugar
- Dash pepper
- 1/2 cup white vinegar
- 1 pint cherry tomatoes, halved
- 1 small cucumber, thinly sliced
- 1 small green pepper, diced
- 1 small onion, diced
- 1 carrot, grated
- 1 stalk celery, sliced

Mix first 5 ingredients together. Combine vegetables in glass serving bowl. Toss gently with dressing. Marinate overnight.

Eggnog Salad

- 1 1-pound can fruit cocktail
- 2 envelopes unflavored gelatin
- 1 11-ounce can mandarin oranges, chopped
- 1/2 cup maraschino cherries, cut up
- 1 cup coconut
- 2½ cups eggnog
- Dash of nutmeg

Drain fruit, saving juice. Add gelatin to juice and stir to dissolve. Combine gelatin with remaining ingredients. Pour into a greased 5-cup mold and chill until firm. Serves 6.

Pineapple Salad

Cut pineapple in half lengthwise through the leaves, retaining leaves. With a grapefruit knife, cut out pineapple pulp. Remove core and slice pineapple in small pieces. Place pineapple and other fruits, such as strawberries, grapes, and melon into shell. In center, place one large scoop of orange sherbet and surround with fruit. Substitute cottage cheese for sherbet, if desired. Serves 2.

Orange-Avocado Salad

- 1 avocado, sliced
- 2 oranges, peeled and sectioned
- 1/4 cup diced red onion
- Red-tipped leaf lettuce

Arrange avocado and orange slices on lettuce. Sprinkle with onion. Serve with a clear dressing such as Italian. Serves 4.

Jellied Loaf

- 4 cups chicken stock
- 3 cups shredded, cooked chicken
- 1/2 cup sugar
- 1/2 cup cider vinegar
- 1/2 cup celery, thinly sliced
- 1 green pepper, thinly sliced
- 1/2 cup sliced green salad olives
- 1/4 teaspoon pepper
- 1 teaspoon seasoned salt
- 1 teaspoon Worcestershire sauce
- 4 tablespoons unflavored gelatin, softened in 1/4 cup cold water
- Lettuce leaves
- Mayonnaise

Place all ingredients except lettuce and mayonnaise in boiling chicken stock. Simmer for 25 minutes. Pour in a large greased or oiled loaf pan or 2 small ones. Place in refrigerator. When well-chilled and firm, unmold, and slice. Place slices on lettuce leaf and garnish with mayonnaise. Serves 4 to 6.

Avocado Stuffed with Chicken

- 2 avocados
- 2 cups diced cooked chicken
- 1 cup diced celery
- 3/4 cup mayonnaise
- 1 teaspoon lemon juice
- 1/4 teaspoon salt
- 1/8 teaspoon pepper
- 1/4 cup sweet relish
- Lettuce leaves
- Shredded lettuce
- Hard-boiled eggs, shelled and sliced
- Tomatoes, sliced
- Olives

Cut avocados lengthwise in half. Peel and place in salt water for a few minutes, or dip in lemon juice so that avocado does not turn dark. Mix chicken, celery, mayonnaise, lemon juice, salt, pepper, and relish together. Fill avocado with mixture. Top with a small piece of chicken. Place on a lettuce leaf with shredded lettuce and garnish with hard-boiled egg slices, olives, and tomato. Serves 4.

Deluxe Potato Salad

 8 medium-size new potatoes
 1 10½-ounce can bouillon
 1 large red onion, finely chopped
12 cherry tomatoes
 1 4-ounce can artichoke hearts, drained and sliced
 4 hard-boiled eggs, chopped
   Chopped parsley
   Salt and pepper
 1 cup mayonnaise

Boil the potatoes in their jackets until tender, about 25 minutes. Drain. When cool, peel and slice. Marinate potato slices in the bouillon for 1 hour. Put onion, cherry tomatoes, artichoke hearts, and eggs, sprinkled with chopped parsley, salt, and pepper into a bowl. Just before serving, drain the potatoes, add to vegetables, and stir in mayonnaise.

Texas Cole Slaw

 1 head green cabbage, shredded
 1 large green pepper, thinly sliced
 1 large onion, thinly sliced
½ cup sugar
 1 cup cider vinegar
 1 tablespoon sugar
1½ teaspoons celery seed
 2 tablespoons dry mustard
 1 cup vegetable oil

Sprinkle cabbage, pepper, and onion with ½ cup sugar and toss. Set aside. In a saucepan, combine vinegar, 1 tablespoon sugar, celery seed, and dry mustard, and bring to a boil. Remove from heat and stir in oil. Bring to a boil again. Pour boiling mixture over cabbage mixture. Toss several times. Cover and refrigerate overnight. Before serving, drain well. May be prepared a day ahead.

Nutty Pear Salad

3 tablespoons vegetable oil
  Juice of 1 large lemon
3 fresh pears, peeled and quartered
1 large head iceberg lettuce, torn into pieces
¾ cup chopped walnuts

Heat oil and juice together; do not boil. Mix pears, nuts, and lettuce together; toss gently. Pour oil and lemon mixture over all. Chill and serve. Serves 6.

Bing Cherry Salad

1 cup pitted bing cherries
1 cup crushed pineapple
1 3-ounce package black cherry gelatin
1 cup chopped pecans or walnuts
1 cup marshmallows, finely chopped
  Lettuce
  Whipped cream

Drain juice from cherries and pineapple. Bring to a boil and add to gelatin. Stir until dissolved. Cool and add fruit, nuts, and marshmallows. Chill until firm. Unmold on a bed of lettuce and top with whipped cream.

Chicken Potato Salad

 4 cups boiled potatoes, diced
 2 cups chicken, diced
1½ cups celery, diced
 1 tablespoon lemon juice
½ teaspoon salt
¼ teaspoon pepper
 1 tablespoon Worcestershire sauce
1½ cups mayonnaise
½ cup pickle relish
  Lettuce leaves
  Shredded lettuce
  Hard-boiled eggs, shelled and sliced
  Olives
  Tomatoes, cut in wedges

Mix first nine ingredients together and chill well. Place on a lettuce leaf and shredded lettuce. Garnish with hard-boiled egg slices, olives, and tomato, if desired. Serves 6.

Chicken and Macaroni Salad

 1 7-ounce package ring macaroni
 1 cup cubed, cooked chicken
 1 cup diced celery
 2 teaspoons chopped parsley
1¼ cups mayonnaise
 1 tablespoon sugar
 1 cup diced apple or pineapple
½ cup chopped nuts, optional
 1 teaspoon salt
½ cup pickle relish, drained
  Lettuce leaves
  Hard-boiled eggs, shelled and sliced
  Green olives

Cook macaroni until just tender. Rinse with cold water. Drain. Gently mix with other ingredients and place on lettuce. Garnish with hard-boiled egg slices and olives. Serves 6.

Salads and Dressings

Ambrosia

- 4 oranges, peeled and cubed
- 3 bananas, sliced
  Lemon juice
- 1 cup walnuts
- 1 cup coconut
- ½ cup cherries, cut in half
- ¼ cup sugar

Sprinkle sliced bananas with lemon juice to prevent them from turning dark. Combine oranges, bananas, walnuts, coconut, and cherries. Add sugar and mix gently. Serves 8 to 10.

Fruit Dressing

- 2 cups mayonnaise
- 2 cups currant jelly
- ¼ cup lemon juice

Blend together all ingredients to make a smooth dressing. Orange or pineapple marmalade may be substituted for currant jelly.

Roquefort Dressing

- 3 cups mayonnaise
- 3 cups sour cream
- 2 tablespoons wine vinegar
- 2 tablespoons lemon juice
- 1 tablespoon Worcestershire sauce
- 2 to 3 dashes Tabasco sauce
- ¼ teaspoon garlic powder
- ¼ cup buttermilk
- 4 to 6 ounces Roquefort or blue cheese, crumbled coarsely

Blend together all ingredients in a large bowl, adding cheese last. Pour into a jar and refrigerate. This is a very good dressing even without adding cheese. Store in the refrigerator. This recipe can be divided in half.

Sweet and Sour Dressing

- 1 cup sugar
- 1 cup vinegar
- 1 cup vegetable oil
- 1 teaspoon seasoned salt
- ½ teaspoon crushed black pepper
- ½ cup minced onion
- ½ cup minced celery
- ¼ cup minced pimiento
- ½ cup minced green pepper
- ¼ cup finely chopped parsley

Combine all ingredients. Refrigerate overnight. Use for tossed green salad.

Thousand Island Dressing

- 3 cups mayonnaise
- 1 cup chili sauce
- ¼ cup grated carrots
- ¼ cup diced ripe olives
- ¼ cup sweet relish
- ¼ cup chopped green pepper
- ⅓ cup chopped beets, including about
  1 tablespoon of liquid

Combine all ingredients and mix thoroughly. Makes 5 to 6 cups.

Old-Fashioned French Dressing

- 2 cups vegetable oil
- 1 cup wine vinegar
- ½ cup sugar
  Dash of dry mustard
- ¼ teaspoon pepper
- 2 teaspoons paprika
- ½ cup catsup
- 1 teaspoon salt

Combine all ingredients in a bottle and shake well. For extra flavor, add 2 tablespoons of one of the following, according to your preference: chopped watercress, chopped anchovies, chopped chives, diced green pepper, diced hard-boiled egg, Parmesan cheese, beaten egg, sliced almonds, chopped parsley, sour cream, grated Cheddar cheese, diced pimiento, or chopped stuffed green olives.

Goddess Dressing

- 2 cups chicken stock
- ½ cup wine vinegar
- 1 tablespoon seasoned salt
- 2 tablespoons sugar
- 2 dashes Tabasco sauce
- 1 clove garlic, minced
- 1 tablespoon Worcestershire sauce
- 4 tablespoons cornstarch mixed with
  4 tablespoons water
- 2 cups mayonnaise
  Spinach juice or green food coloring
  Anchovies, chopped

Bring chicken stock, vinegar, seasoned salt, sugar, Tabasco sauce, garlic, and Worcestershire sauce to a boil. Whip in cornstarch mixture and let simmer for 3 to 4 minutes. Remove from heat. Cool for 5 minutes, then whip in mayonnaise. A little spinach juice or green food coloring gives this a pretty tint. Refrigerate and use for salads or baked potatoes. Chopped anchovies may be used as a garnish. Makes 3 cups.

Accompaniments

Spicy Corn Bread

    3 strips bacon, diced
    ½ green pepper, diced
    ½ onion, diced
    2 tablespoons butter
 1½ cups flour
    1 cup cornmeal
    3 tablespoons sugar
    1 teaspoon salt
 3½ teaspoons baking powder
    2 eggs
 2½ cups buttermilk

Sauté bacon, pepper and onion in butter. Mix flour, cornmeal, sugar, salt, and baking powder together. Add sautéed mixture to eggs then add dry ingredients alternately with buttermilk and mix well. Pour into a greased 8 x 8-inch baking pan and bake for 40 minutes in a 375° oven.

Corn Fritters

    2 cups flour
    3 teaspoons baking powder
    1 teaspoon salt
    2 eggs, beaten
    1 cup milk
    2 tablespoons butter or margarine, melted
 1½ cups whole kernel corn, drained
       Vegetable oil for frying

Sift flour, baking powder, and salt together. Blend eggs, milk, and butter together. Mix with dry ingredients. Add corn and drop by spoonfuls into 250° oil in an electric skillet. Serves 8.

Three-Flavor Biscuits

    2 cups flour
    1 tablespoon baking powder
    1 teaspoon salt
    ¼ cup shortening
    5 slices crisp bacon, drained and crumbled
    ½ cup shredded Cheddar cheese
    ¼ cup finely chopped scallions
    ½ to ¾ cup milk

Sift together flour, baking powder and salt. Cut in shortening until mixture resembles coarse crumbs. Add bacon, cheese and scallions. Blend in enough milk to make a soft dough. Turn onto a lightly floured surface and knead gently 30 seconds. Roll out ½ inch thick and cut with a lightly floured biscuit cutter. Place on ungreased baking sheet. Bake in a 450° oven 10 to 12 minutes or until lightly browned. Makes 12 biscuits.

Easy Popovers

    3 eggs
    1 cup milk
    1 tablespoon butter, melted
    1 cup sifted flour
    ½ teaspoon seasoned salt

Beat eggs. Add milk and melted butter. Beat well. Add sifted flour and seasoned salt. Beat until smooth. Pour batter into well-greased muffin tins. Bake in a 450° oven for 20 minutes. Reduce heat to 350° and bake for 25 minutes more. Serve while hot. Makes 11 popovers.

Sweet Potato Biscuits

    1 teaspoon salt
    2 cups flour
    4 teaspoons baking powder
    3 tablespoons butter
    1 cup mashed sweet potatoes
    ¾ cup milk, approximately

Sift salt, flour, and baking powder together. Cut in butter until mixture resembles crumbs. Add sweet potatoes and enough milk to form dough. Roll out dough on floured board to ½-inch thickness. Cut biscuits with small, round cookie cutter. Place on greased baking sheet and bake in a 375° oven for 14 minutes or until golden brown. Makes 1½ dozen.

Pineapple-Nut Bread

 2½ cups sifted flour
    1 tablespoon baking powder
    ½ teaspoon baking soda
    1 teaspoon salt
    ½ teaspoon cinnamon
    2 tablespoons butter, softened
 1¼ cups sugar
    3 eggs
    1 tablespoon lemon juice
    2 cups crushed pineapple with juice
    ½ cup chopped nuts

Sift together flour, baking powder, baking soda, salt, and cinnamon. Cream butter and sugar thoroughly in a large mixing bowl. Beat in eggs. Stir in lemon juice, pineapple with juice, and nuts. Add flour mixture all at once and stir until dry ingredients are moistened. Turn into a well-greased loaf pan (8½ x 4½ x 2¾ inches) and bake in a 375° oven about 1 hour. Cool in pan for 5 minutes, then turn out on rack. Makes 1 loaf.

Rice Pilaf

    ½ cup diced onion
    1 cup diced mushrooms
    3 tablespoons butter or margarine
    1 cup converted, long grain rice
    1 tablespoon chopped parsley
    2 cups chicken stock
    1 teaspoon salt

Sauté onion and mushrooms in butter lightly. Add rice and parsley and mix well. Stir in chicken stock and salt. Bring to a boil. Cover and let simmer for 15 minutes. Turn off heat and let stand, covered, for 15 minutes. Fluff and serve. Yield: 3 cups.

All-Purpose Stuffing

    1 egg
    2 cups milk or chicken stock
    ½ loaf dry bread, cubed
    1 cup diced onion
    1 cup diced celery
    ½ cup margarine
    1 cup diced apple
    ½ teaspoon salt
    ¼ teaspoon pepper
    ¼ teaspoon poultry seasoning
    2 tablespoons chopped parsley

Beat egg with milk and pour over dry bread cubes. Set aside. Sauté onion and celery in margarine for 3 to 4 minutes. Add remaining ingredients to bread cubes and add sautéed onion and celery. Mix well.

Bran Muffins

    1 cup boiling water
    2½ teaspoons baking soda
    ½ cup shortening
    1 cup sugar
    1 egg
    1 egg yolk
    2 cups buttermilk
    2½ cups flour
    ½ teaspoon salt
    2 cups all-bran cereal
    ½ cup chopped nuts
    1 cup chopped dates or raisins

Dissolve soda in boiling water; cool. Cream shortening and sugar together. Add water and 1 egg, beating well. Stir in remaining ingredients in order given, beating well after each addition. Store in refrigerator overnight or up to six weeks. Bake at 375° for 20 minutes. Makes 3 dozen muffins.

Banana Bread

    1 cup sugar
    ½ cup butter or margarine, softened
    1 teaspoon baking soda
    1 tablespoon sour milk or orange juice
    2 eggs, well beaten
    3 ripe bananas, mashed
    2 cups flour
    ¼ cup chopped nuts

Cream butter and sugar together. Stir soda into sour milk or orange juice. Add eggs, bananas, soda mixture, and flour to butter mixture, beating thoroughly. Stir in nuts. Pour into a buttered 9 x 5 x 3-inch bread pan. Bake at 350° for 1 hour. Serve with chicken salad.

Egg Bread

    4 to 4½ cups all-purpose flour
    2 packages dry yeast
    2 tablespoons sugar
    2 teaspoons salt
    ½ cup water
    ½ cup milk
    2 tablespoons shortening
    3 eggs, slightly beaten (save 1 tablespoon for glaze)

In large mixing bowl, combine 2 cups flour, yeast, sugar, and salt; mix well. In saucepan, heat water, milk, and shortening until warm (shortening does not need to melt); add to flour mixture. Add eggs. Blend at low speed until moistened; beat 3 minutes at medium speed. Gradually stir in remaining flour by hand to make a firm dough. Knead on floured board until smooth and elastic, about 5 minutes. Place in greased bowl, turning to grease top. Cover; let rise in warm place until double in bulk, about 1 hour. Punch down dough; divide into 3 equal parts. Roll each part on lightly floured board to make a 15-inch strand. On greased baking sheet, braid loosely. Pinch ends and tuck under to seal. Cover; let rise in warm place until doubled in bulk, about 30 minutes. Brush with reserved egg. Bake in preheated 400° oven 25 to 30 minutes or until golden brown. Cool.

Herb Bread Crumbs

    1 cup bread crumbs
    ¼ teaspoon oregano leaves
    ½ teaspoon sweet basil
    ⅛ teaspoon garlic powder

Mix all ingredients together.

Dilly Bread

    1 package compressed yeast
    ¼ cup warm water
    1 cup creamed cottage cheese, small curd
    2¼ cups flour
    2 tablespoons sugar
    1 teaspoon minced onion
    2 tablespoons dill seed
    1 teaspoon salt
    ¼ teaspoon baking soda
      Melted butter
      Salt

Dissolve yeast in ¼ cup warm water. Heat the cottage cheese until lukewarm, then combine with dissolved yeast and flour. Add remaining ingredients and beat well. Pour into well-buttered 9 x 5 x 3-inch bread pan and allow to rise until doubled in bulk. Brush top with melted butter and sprinkle with salt. Bake at 350° for 40 to 45 minutes. Use for chicken or turkey sandwiches.

Stuffed Baked Potatoes

    4 baking potatoes
      Salt to taste
    1 cup sour cream
    4 teaspoons chopped chives or green onion
    4 slices bacon, fried crisp and crumbled
    4 teaspoons butter or margarine
      Paprika

Bake potatoes in a 400° oven until tender, about 50 minutes. Cool for 5 minutes. Cut across top of potato lengthwise. Remove potato without breaking skin. Mash and salt to taste. Add sour cream, chives, and bacon. Put mixture back into skin. Add teaspoon of butter to each and sprinkle with paprika. Return to the oven for 20 minutes at 350°. Potatoes may be stored in the refrigerator until ready to reheat. Reheat in a 350° oven for 30 minutes. Serves 4.

Sprinkle potato slices lightly with flour prior to frying for a crisp, golden appearance.

Oven Brown Potatoes

    6 medium potatoes
    3 tablespoons vegetable oil
      Salt
      Paprika

Peel potatoes. Brush with 1½ tablespoons oil. Sprinkle with salt and paprika. Brush with remaining 1½ tablespoons oil. Place in a baking pan and bake for 45 minutes in a 375° oven until brown. Serves 6.

Cranberry-Nut Bread

    1 cup cranberries, coarsely chopped
    1 cup sugar
    3 cups sifted all-purpose flour
    1 tablespoon baking powder
    1 teaspoon salt
    ½ cup chopped walnuts
      Rind of 1 orange, grated
    3 eggs
    1¼ cups milk
    4 tablespoons butter, melted

Mix cranberries with ¼ cup sugar and set aside. Sift remaining sugar, flour, baking powder, and salt together. Add nuts and orange rind. Beat eggs slightly and combine with milk and butter. Add to dry ingredients and mix well. Fold in cranberries and pour into a buttered loaf pan (8½ x 4½ x 2¾ inches). Bake in a 350° oven for 1 hour.

Summer Vegetable Medley

    2 cups hot water
    1 tablespoon salt
    2 teaspoons sugar
    ¼ teaspoon white pepper
    6 ears corn, broken into thirds
    1 pound green beans
    2 medium green peppers, cut into squares
    2 stalks celery, cut into 1-inch pieces
    1 large red onion, cut into wedges
    2 large tomatoes, cut into wedges

In a large saucepan, bring water, salt, sugar, and pepper to a boil. Add corn; boil 5 minutes. Add green beans; boil 5 minutes. Add peppers and celery; boil 1 minute. With a slotted spoon, transfer vegetables to a serving platter. Arrange onion and tomatoes on top.

Sautéed Buttered Noodles, page 28
Vegetables and Brown Rice, page 33
Stuffed Baked Potatoes

Accompaniments

Noodles with Cinnamon

1 16-ounce package medium-size egg noodles
6 eggs, beaten
½ cup sugar
1 teaspoon cinnamon
1 1-pound creamed cottage cheese, large curd
½ cup margarine, melted
½ teaspoon salt

Cook noodles according to package directions and drain. Rinse with cold water. Add sugar and cinnamon to eggs. Combine with noodles, cottage cheese, margarine, and salt. Pour into a greased 9 x 13 x 1-inch pan. Bake at 350° for 45 minutes, or until golden.

Oven Mashed Potatoes

4 cups mashed potatoes, seasoned to taste
1 cup shredded Cheddar cheese
3 tablespoons margarine
Paprika
Parsley

This recipe can be made ahead of time, refrigerated, and baked when needed. Place mashed potatoes in a baking dish and sprinkle with cheese. Dot with margarine and sprinkle with paprika and parsley. Bake, covered, in a 350° oven for about 1 hour until potatoes are heated through. Remove cover last 10 minutes to allow potatoes to brown lightly. Serves 4 to 6.

Baked Bean Pot

1 pound dried beans (kidney, navy, lima, or a combination)
2 tablespoons vegetable oil
1 large onion, chopped
1 green pepper, chopped
¼ pound bacon, diced
2 teaspoons salt
1 1-pound can tomatoes, broken
2 tablespoons brown sugar
2 teaspoons prepared mustard
½ teaspoon Tabasco sauce
½ teaspoon Worcestershire sauce

Place beans in a large saucepan and cover with water. Bring to a boil, reduce heat and cover. Simmer about 1 hour. In a small skillet, sauté onion and green pepper in oil for 5 minutes. Add with remaining ingredients to beans. Cover and simmer 1 hour more. Stir frequently. Add water, if needed, during cooking. May be prepared ahead and refrigerated.

Garlic Bread

1 loaf Italian or French bread
½ cup butter, softened
1 clove garlic, minced
½ teaspoon oregano, crushed
½ teaspoon dried dill weed, crushed

Cut bread crosswise into 1-inch slices. Blend butter, garlic, oregano, and dill weed together. Spread over slices of bread. Put slices together in original shape; wrap in foil. Bake in a preheated 400° oven for 15 to 20 minutes or until bread is heated through. Bread may be spread with butter mixture, wrapped, and chilled until ready to bake.

Corn Pudding

2 1-pound cans corn, drained
3 eggs
1½ cups milk
2 teaspoons sugar
1 tablespoon butter, melted
1 teaspoon salt
1 teaspoon pepper
6 slices bacon

Beat eggs well. Add milk, sugar, butter, seasonings, and corn. Pour into a 1½-quart greased baking dish. Lay bacon strips across top. Bake at 350° for 45 to 50 minutes, or until firm. Serves 6 to 8.

Sweet Potato Casserole

8 sweet potatoes, pared and cut up
¼ teaspoon nutmeg
½ teaspoon cinnamon
¼ teaspoon salt
4 tablespoons vegetable oil
⅓ cup sugar
⅓ cup dark brown sugar
14 large marshmallows
½ cup pecan halves

Boil sweet potatoes for 30 minutes, or until tender. Mash. Add remaining ingredients, except marshmallows and pecans. Spoon mixture into greased casserole, cover with marshmallows, and sprinkle with pecan halves. Bake at 350° for 30 minutes. Serve immediately.

Sauces

Old-World Cranberry Sauce

2 cups brown sugar
2 cups orange juice
4 cups cranberries (1 pound)
1 cup pecans, optional
1 tablespoon chutney

Boil sugar and orange juice in a large saucepan. Add cranberries and boil 4 minutes until skins pop. Remove from heat and set aside to cool. Add pecans and chutney. Makes a delicious sauce for any type of meat or wild game. Makes 1 to 1½ quarts.

Cheese Sauce

3 tablespoons butter or margarine
3 tablespoons flour
2½ cups milk *or* 1½ cups milk and 1 cup chicken stock
½ teaspoon salt
Drop of Tabasco sauce
1 teaspoon Worcestershire sauce
1 cup shredded Cheddar cheese

Melt butter in a medium-size saucepan. Add flour and mix well. Cook over low heat for 1 to 2 minutes. Add milk or milk-chicken stock mixture. Blend with wire whisk until thick and smooth. Add salt, Tabasco, Worcestershire sauce, and Cheddar cheese. Mix well. Serve over baked potatoes or mix in mashed potatoes with chives. This can be used for macaroni and cheese, over fish, eggs, or whenever a cheese sauce needed.

Barbecue Sauce for Chicken

¼ cup vegetable oil
1 medium onion, diced
1 tablespoon flour
2 1-pound cans tomato purée
2 cups chicken stock
1 cup brown sugar
½ cup vinegar
1 tablespoon seasoned salt
1 clove garlic, minced
2 tablespoons liquid smoke
1 tablespoon Worcestershire sauce
½ tablespoon Tabasco sauce

Heat oil in large pot; add onion and sauté for 3 minutes. Add flour, mixing well, then add all other ingredients. Simmer for 1 hour, stirring occasionally to prevent sticking. Refrigerate until needed, up to 2 weeks.

Piquant Tomato Sauce

2 cups water
½ cup vegetable or olive oil
1 large onion, minced
2 cloves garlic, minced
1 1-pound can tomatoes
1 1-pound can tomato sauce
½ cup wine vinegar
½ cup sugar
1 teaspoon sweet basil
1 teaspoon oregano
2 teaspoons salt
¼ teaspoon pepper
½ cup chopped parsley

In a large pot, combine water, oil, onion, and garlic and simmer for 3 minutes. Add all other ingredients and simmer 1 hour. This sauce is good on any type of fish, chicken, meat loaf, macaroni, or spaghetti.

Basic White Sauce

3 tablespoons butter
3 tablespoons flour
2 cups milk or light cream, scalded
½ teaspoon salt
¼ teaspoon white pepper
1 or 2 egg yolks, optional

Melt butter in a small saucepan; add flour. Cook over low heat for 1 to 2 minutes, stirring constantly. Add scalded milk and keep stirring until thick and smooth. Add seasonings and simmer a few minutes. To enrich White Sauce, combine 1 or 2 egg yolks with 1 tablespoon sauce and add, beating well, while sauce is hot. Do not boil. You may thin sauce to desired consistency by adding a little hot milk or cream. This sauce can be used whenever cream sauce is called for, such as in ala king, macaroni and cheese, creamed soups, newburgs, or cheese sauce.

Desserts

Orange Cake

  8 eggs, separated
1⅓ cups sugar
  ½ teaspoon salt
  1 cup flour
    Rind of 1 orange
  ¼ cup orange juice

Beat egg yolks with ⅔ cup sugar and salt. Combine flour and orange rind; add to egg yolk mixture alternately with orange juice. Beat egg whites with remaining sugar and fold gently into first mixture. Bake in ungreased angel food cake pan for 1 hour at 325°.

Basic Pie Crust

  ½ teaspoon salt
  2 cups all-purpose flour
  ⅔ cup shortening
  6 tablespoons ice water

Sift salt and flour together. Cut in shortening with a pastry blender until mixture looks like coarse cornmeal. Add enough ice water to hold mixture together. Roll out on a floured board. Makes pastry for 1 double-crust 9-inch pie.

Sour Cream Fruit Pie

  ½ cup fruit juice or water
  ½ cup brown sugar
  1 3-ounce package lime or lemon gelatin
  1 cup sour cream
  2 cups fruit (green grapes, bananas, strawberries and/or canned pineapple, drained)
  1 9-inch pie shell, baked
    Whipped cream
    Nuts

Pour juice over bananas to keep them from turning dark. Drain juice into a saucepan. Bring juice and brown sugar to a boil. When sugar is dissolved, add gelatin. When gelatin has dissolved, remove from heat and cool several minutes. Whip in sour cream and fold in fruit. Pour into pie shell and chill well. Top with whipped cream and sprinkle with nuts.

To keep pie crust from getting soggy, before filling, brush sides and bottom with beaten egg white. Place in a 375° oven for about 4 minutes. Then fill and bake per recipe.

Apple Caramel Pie

  6 apples, cored and sliced
  1 9-inch deep-dish pie shell, unbaked
  ½ cup butter, softened
  ½ cup flour
1½ cups brown sugar
  ¼ teaspoon cinnamon
  1 cup chopped walnuts
    Whipped cream

Arrange apple slices in pie shell. Mix butter, flour, brown sugar, salt, and cinnamon. Spread mixture over apples and sprinkle with walnuts. Bake in a 350° oven for 50 minutes. Serve with whipped cream.

Cranberry Pie

  1 9-inch pie shell, baked
  1 pound fresh cranberries
  1 6½-ounce can pineapple chunks, drained
  1 cup pineapple juice
  2 cups sugar
    Juice of 1 lemon
  2 tablespoons unflavored gelatin
    Whipped cream
    Chopped nuts

Bring all ingredients to a boil, except pie shell, whipped cream and nuts, for 10 minutes. Cool. Pour into pie shell and chill. Cover with whipped cream and sprinkle with chopped nuts.

Rice Pudding

  6 eggs, beaten
1½ cups sugar
  4 cups milk
  1 teaspoon cinnamon
  ½ teaspoon salt
  2 tablespoons butter or margarine, melted
  ½ teaspoon nutmeg
  1 teaspoon vanilla
  1 drop yellow food coloring
  2 cups cooked rice
  1 cup raisins
    Whipped cream

Combine first nine ingredients. Stir in rice and raisins. Mix well. Pour into a greased baking dish and bake in a 350° oven for 50 minutes. Chill and top with whipped cream. Serves 4.

Variation: ½ cup chopped nuts and ½ cup pineapple may be added for extra flavor.

Index

E F G H I J K L   4 5 6 7 8 9 0 1

Cover Recipe: Chicken in Beer Batter, page 6;
Three-Flavor Biscuits, page 56;
Summer Vegetable Medley, page 59